A SPIRITUAL GUIDE
FOR ALL
NEW BELIEVERS IN CHRIST JESUS

Culbert Delisle Blenman

JAKO BOOKS

Vieux Fort, New York, London

To order additional copies of this book, contact Culbert Delisle Blenman at:

Email: c.blennman@gmail.com

Telephone: 1-758-454-7140;

Cell: 1-758-722-4901

Library of Congress Control Number (LCCN)

2021937488

ISBN

paperback: 978-1-7332913-4-7

eBook: 978-1-7332913-5-4

THE AWESOME POWERS OF THE REDEEMED
AND
RIGHTEOUS HUMAN SOUL ON FIRE FOR GOD

BE ENCOURAGED BY THESE VERSES OF HOLY SPIRIT INSPIRATION, WHEN YOU PUT YOUR HANDS TO THE PLOW TO WORK FOR GOD:

"King David said to his son Solomon, 'Be confident and determined. Start the work, [God's work], and don't let anything stop you. The Lord your God whom I serve will be with you. He will not abandon you, but he will stay with you until you finish the work to be done…" (1 Chron. 28:20, GNB).

"Not by [human] might nor by [human] power, but by my spirit, [God's supernatural power], says the Lord Almighty" (Zechariah 4:6, NIV).

For Jesus said In Luke 10:19, "Behold, I give you power to tread on serpents and scorpions, and over all the power of the enemy [Satan]; and nothing shall by no means hurt you."

Also by Culbert Delisle Blenman

In Pursuit of Happiness, Peace, and Joy, through the Wisdom of the Kingdom, the Power and the Glory

Character Building through Christian Education, For Youth (Volumes 1 & 2)

A Spiritual Guide for Choosing a Suitable Christian Companion and Helpmate for Marriage

DEDICATION

To the honor and glory of Almighty God: for the salvation of every newly redeemed and righteous born-again-believer in Christ Jesus, and all the unrighteous and backsliders.

MY PRAYER

Dear God, give me an enthusiastic spirit to always be spiritually on fire for Jesus, (through the power of the Holy Spirit), and to have a faith in Him that is contagious; so that all persons who read this inspirational handbook will eventually be saved, and experience Your love, joy, peace, grace, mercy, protection, and provision, through the power of Jesus Christ and the Holy Spirit—as the power of salvation and our final hope for eternal life, for celestial glory. This is my humble prayer, in the powerful and awesome name of your dearly beloved Son (Jesus Christ), Amen.

We receive salvation and eternal life through our faith in Jesus Christ, and God's generous dispensation of undeserved favor of grace and mercy to us—not by our good works alone; for our righteous acts are like filthy rags, says Isaiah 64:6.

Salvation and eternal life are God's free gifts to us, when we repent of our sin (or sins), and accept Jesus Christ as our lord and personal savior. And they are free for the asking and the taking.

They are God's earthly and celestial spiritual power-package of "abundant life," for all the redeemed and the righteous, through the power of Christ Jesus and the Holy Spirit.

CONTENTS

A SPECIAL NOTE FROM THE AUTHOR

All Scripture quotations marked NKJV are from the New Authorized King James Version, World Bible Publishers, USA, 1978.

The scripture quotations marked NIV are taken from the Holy Bible (New International Version Study Bible), Copyright © USA, 1965, 1973, 1978 and 1984, by the International Bible Society.

The "Good News Bible" quotations marked GNB, are taken from the Good News Translation of the American Bible Society, Copyright © 1966, 1971, 1976 and 1979. Be mindful also, that the Good News Bible quotations which I occasionally use in this handbook, are the same as in the Old King James Version Bible, marked OKJV (Authorized Version), first published in 1611, Copyright © 1983, by the Zondervan Corporation.

The meanings of all words and phrases in single and double open and closed quotation marks, followed by an asterisk (*), will be found in the Glossary and phrase list. And some biblical quotations have been repeatedly used to emphasize similarly related ideas, or situations, in different chapters.

Furthermore, to facilitate and familiarize new believers with the spellings of the names of the different books of the Holy Bible, I have spelled them out fully after each quotation—instead of using their abbreviations. For example, I use the full names or spellings of "James" and "John" for each book, instead of the shortened form of "Jas" and "Jn" respectively. And in some instances, I have expanded some definitions so that the new believer or convert could get better understanding.

Also, if the new convert or believer does not comprehend the simple and basic truths of Jesus Christ's gospel message for our "redemption"* and "salvation,"* (after having had water baptism and participating in new converts' classes), he or she is not truly "born-again,"* or a "new creation"* (2 Corinthians 5:17): which means, he is still in darkness and not spiritually transformed to some extent, and has not received the Holy Spirit. So the gospel message of the cross and our crucified, dead, buried, and risen Savior, is also incomprehensive and foolishness to him. Consequently, Satan's temptations and persecutions may even be too strong or difficult for him to handle at that time, and he may backslide. Be ever mindful also, that it is or may not be too early or impossible for the new convert or believer to backslide, a few weeks or months after he or she has made his or her profession of faith in Christ Jesus. Pre-supposing and anticipating this situation, I have summoned the power of the Holy Spirit through prayer, to remove the cloud of darkness from the mind of every new convert who read this manual; so that he or she can read and understand, and retain and recall when necessary—for the use of protection, strength, and guidance—God's appropriate biblically hidden truths in this manual, extracted from the Holy Bible. Otherwise, Satan will instigate spiritual confusion, as well as doubt, fear, depression and defeat, in the new believer's mind. And he or she will easily forfeit the precious gift of salvation. This phenomenon can be better understood by reading "the Parable of the Sower," in Matthew Chapter 13:1-23, (more clearly explained in lines 16 to 21), and "the Parable of the Weeds," in Matthew Chapter 13:24-30, more clearly explained also, in lines 37-43.

This handbook will inform and teach the new believer how he or she can completely surrender his or her life to Jesus, after first repentance, so that he or she will become strong and victorious over Satan. And consequently also, how by daily continual submission, with obedience, prayer, meditation, and faithfulness to Christ Jesus, (whilst trusting Him "as our Lord and Personal Savior," and renouncing all Satan's works and promises), this can easily happen. Jesus says, in John 14:1: "Do not let your hearts be troubled. Trust in God; trust also in me." And St. Paul says, in 1 Thessalonians 5:23, "May the God of peace himself sanctify you wholly; and may your spirit and soul and body be kept sound." So that by the time you finish reading this handbook, you will be equipped to answer these questions:

(1) What is the Christian life all about? Or what are you getting into?

(2) What quality of life does God expect from you and me as a believer?

(3) What should be a believer's Christian life coping skills?

(4) What are God's earthly blessings for enduring your daily spiritual struggles?

(5) And what are God's eternal heavenly rewards for living righteously on earth.

I have tried my best to reveal with clarity, sincerity, simplicity, honesty, and humility, in this manual, most of the important information that a new believer needs to know to encourage, secure, and protect his and other believers salvation, or his or her own born-again godly-life, in and through Christ Jesus. I hope he or she will appreciate this little helpful treat, and give Almighty God all the honor, praise and glory, that He rightly deserves.

"Blessed be His holy name!"

FOREWORD

For you to clearly understand the expression: "The Awesome Powers of The Redeemed and The Righteous Human Soul on Fire for God," it is very important for me to define what the human soul is, and its attributes (or characteristics), when on fire for God. The Winston Senior Dictionary says that the soul is:

"The spiritual, immaterial, and immortal part in man, as distinguished from the body: that part of man's nature where feelings, ideals, and morals center; that part that gives vigor and character [to man]."

But be forever mindful, that the Holy Scriptures say in Ezekiel 18:4 and 18:20, "The soul who sins is the one who will die."

So the human soul is definitely not immortal after all, as stated in the Winston Senior Dictionary's definition above.

Holy Scriptures always and only speaks "The Truth,"* because it was inspired by God and the Holy Spirit. Therefore, it was inspired or spiritually empowered men of God who wrote it. So it is "God's Holy Word," or "The Undiluted Truth." This is as much as I can say for the definition and attributes of the human soul of "the redeemed"* and "the righteous"* on fire for God, and God's Holy Word.

Now what is the awesome power of the redeemed and the righteous human soul on fire for God all about?

It is about the effective, diligent, wise, and active use of God's powerful, spiritually anointed gifts of faith, hope, and love, with the fruit of the Holy Spirit (Galatians 5:22-23); and the power of fasting, fervent prayer and meditation, as well as the awesome use of "the powerful name of Jesus," and "the pleading of His Precious Blood." It also refers to the utilization of God's Holy Word as "a two-edged sword" for Christian defense, edification, preaching, encouragement, teaching, and exhortation and healing, in ministry situations.

Let me now inform you about how a redeemed or righteous human soul becomes awesomely powerful on fire for God:

1. It initially begins when the Holy Spirit first convicts and convinces a sinner of his or her wrong-doing, when he or she hears and listens to God's Holy Word, or God initiates an early call of one righteous person as a child, or one whom He has chosen, claimed, and anointed for kingdom ministry from within his or her mother's womb.

2. So from the point of view of "a convicted sinner"* who has been redeemed and becomes "a born-again believer,"* the process continues through "God's justification"* and "sanctification," with "special anointing"* of "the Christ-redeemed soul"* for "kingdom ministry."* Consequently, a righteous and/or redeemed human soul emerges, spirit-filled and on fire for God through the power of Christ Jesus and the Holy Spirit—just like St. Paul in the New Testament Church of Biblical times. And, as for God's anointing from childhood, the prophet Samuel in 1 Samuel of the Old Testament Biblical era, and the prophet Jeremiah within his mother's womb, mentioned in Jeremiah 1:5 of the Old Testament Biblical era are fitting examples.

3. And finally, the "called," "chosen," "godly-justified,"* "sanctified,"* and "anointed,"* "redeemed"* and "righteous"* human soul on fire for God becomes more zealous and bold in God's "kingdom ministry,"* every day, through the powers and strength of Jesus Christ and the knowledge and power of "God's Holy Word,"* and the power and "fruit of the Holy Spirit."* The awesome power of "fervent prayer,"* "fasting,"* and "meditation"* on Gods Holy Word, also plays an important role in empowering

the believer. That is how a redeemed or a righteous human soul becomes powerfully on fire for God.

Now how do the redeemed and the righteous human soul operate when awesomely on fire for God?

1. He/she speaks continually and very passionately about Jesus Christ as "his/her Lord"* and "Personal Savior,"* and as "The Only Way, Truth, and Life."*

2. He/she teaches all about God's promise of "abundant life"* for all believers, through Christ Jesus (John 10:10), and Jesus Christ's victory over Satan, sin, the fear of death, hell, lack, diseases, and the grave, through His death, burial, resurrection, and ascension into heaven.

3. He/she always upholds "God's Holy Word"* as "The Truth;"*

4. And he/she boldly proclaims "the Good News"* of "Salvation"* and "Eternal life,"* when preaching about the Gospel message of and about Jesus Christ who was crucified, died, was buried, and then resurrected after three days in the tomb; and then He ascended into heaven to prepare a place of eternal rest, peace, joy, happiness, worship, praise, thanksgiving, and rejoicing, for all believers—the righteous and redeemed human souls, dead and alive, who kept faithful to God's promises.

Jesus came on earth so that we would be redeemed from the shackles of sin and condemnation to hell-fire, and enjoy "abundant life"* here on earth and in the hereafter.

This book is also about God's redeeming power, grace, love, and mercy, in and on my life, and the lives of many other divinely chosen contemporary believers, as well as some other righteous and redeemed human souls on fire for Him in the Old and New Testament biblical times; so that my "testimonies"* and "exhortations,"* as well as their stalwart spiritual contribution and performances of "Godly Power," demonstrated through Holy Scripture, can be gratefully recognized, appreciated, enhanced, and embraced, as a tremendous source of encouragement and consolation, for and by all the workers on fire in Almighty God's vineyard.

And, since Revelation 12:11 says that we must overcome the devil "by the blood of the Lamb," (our faith in the power of Jesus Christ's shed-precious-blood on Calvary), and by proclaiming "our testimony," (the truth about what God has done for us), that is also what I seek to do in this hand book—even though I know that Satan already has a plan to discourage me from writing it, for me not to expose his schemes to new converts. But never mind; God will definitely take care of him! So just sit back, relax, and look forward to my godly planned presentation. But, before I do this, let me boldly introduce what August 2nd 1988 issue of "Our Daily Bread" says about God's plan for every redeemed and righteous believer: "When God pardons [our] sin, he purges the record, erases the remembrance, and empowers the recipient [for special and awesome kingdom ministry]."

So I don't have to worry about Satan trying to steal my joy, zeal, and strength anymore, when writing this hand-book; for I have gained victory over him through Christ Jesus, who has set me free. Satan is an already defeated foe!

INTRODUCTION

Even though the awesome powers of the redeemed and/or the righteous human soul on fire for God are very unique, exclusive, seemingly strange, overwhelming, and sometimes very humiliating, they are very rewarding. And they make all the redeemed and the righteous born-again believers in Christ Jesus, by nature, "Fools for Christ,"* says St. Paul. And that is how the world views or sees us also, because darkness does not understand light: "The gospel message is foolishness to them!"

In 1 Corinthians 1:20 in the NIV Bible, St. Paul says, "God chose the foolish things [especially people] of this world to shame the wise, and the weak things of this world to shame the strong."

But some "born-again"* redeemed-believers think more differently and progressively about that; for Jim Elliot (missionary and martyr) said, "He is no fool [God's anointed], who gives what he cannot keep [the Good News of the Lord's Gospel message of salvation and eternal life], to gain what he cannot lose"—the joy, prosperity, and peace of salvation, which the Lord Jesus Christ has to offer us.

In fact, when Jim Elliot said, "[He] gives what he cannot keep to gain what he cannot lose," I think of two passages of Holy Scripture: Jeremiah 20:9, and Mathew 10:39.

Jeremiah 20:9 in the NIV Bible says, "His word is in my heart like a fire, a fire shut up in my bones. I am weary of holding it in; indeed, I cannot."

And Matthew 10:39 in the NIV says, "Whoever finds his life will lose it, and whoever loses his life for my sake will find it," Jesus says.

Like every other born-again redeemed or righteous believer, (including me), Jeremiah, (God's anointed prophet and servant), could not keep "God's Word" in his heart; for his joy, peace, and prosperity through "The Good News of God's Kingdom message" overwhelmed him so much, that he eventually or finally had to tell someone and the whole world about it. And that was a very wise decision he made; because God can make even the stones on the earth preach or do His will, if we refuse to do so (Matthew 3:9). Look at how God used the prophet Balaam's donkey to talk to Balaam for Him, when Balaam attempted to curse Israel and go against God's will (Numbers 22:28-30). Could you imagine a donkey talking to someone for God?

Jeremiah's joy was like that of the woman in Luke 15:8-10, who lost and found her coin, in "the Parable of the Lost Coin," and like the joy of the father in "The Parable of the Lost Son," when his wayward son returned home (Luke 15:11-31). It was as though Jeremiah had found a very great treasure; for his joy was overflowing like the widow's, and the father whose lost son had returned. So he had to share it with friends and strangers, or anyone who cared and wanted to listen to him.

Furthermore, Jim Elliot implied, as in Matthew 10:39, that the giving of one's life to and for Christ Jesus' sake is to save or keep it—or to have "abundant life." For unselfishness, giving, caring, and sharing, always brings back to the giver an abundant reward: "What one cannot lose." And one's storehouses will never be empty but full of all forms of prosperity (or endless blessings).

I repeat what Jesus said in Mathew 10:39 in the GNB Bible: "Whoever tries to gain his life [through selfishness] will lose it; but whoever loses his life [through righteous living] for my sake will gain it."

Therefore, "Our Daily Bread" meditation issue of January 28th 1989 said, that the most powerful ministry on earth is the ministry of the righteous and the redeemed human soul on fire for God. Why? Because through a life of sacrificial love, with faithfulness, habitual and fervent prayer, fasting, preaching, teaching, and a healing ministry, etc., many human souls have been and are being saved every day, for the sake of Jesus Christ and God's Kingdom.

And although many souls are being persecuted and martyred occasionally, thousands of more souls are being saved every day in "open-air crusades"* around the world. Therefore, the angels of God are rejoicing in heaven, as we on earth also rejoice.

January 16th 1989 "Our Daily Bread" meditation issue said, "Satan's ploys are no match for the Savior's power." We only have to read about the lives of great Christians like saints Peter, Paul, and Jesus' other Apostles, as well as St. Stephen in the book of Acts of the New Testament, in the Holy Bible, and other renowned stalwarts like evangelist Billy Graham, Pastor Benny Hinn, Oral Roberts, Mother Teresa, Charles Splurgon, D. L. Moody, John Wesley, etc., to verify this fact. Some are already deceased, and others are still alive, and are being revered today as very powerful, steadfast, and great persons of faith and action, because they have saved many lost souls for Christ Jesus. St. Paul gave an explanation for all these powerful and sacrificial attitudes of courage, fearlessness, and perseverance that he and other redeemed and righteous Christians have maintained in God's kingdom ministry, despite all the threats, executions, and persecutions that they have experienced.

In Romans 8:18 of the NIV Bible, St. Paul said, "I consider that what we suffer at this present time cannot be compared at all to the glory that will be revealed to us [in heaven, or the hereafter]."

And then he (Paul) continued, in Romans 8:28 in the NIV Bible, "And we know that in all things God works for good with those who love him, those whom he has called according to his purpose."

"May God's name be praised and glorified always!"

SOME IMPORTANT EXHORTATIONS
FOR NEW BELIEVERS IN CHRIST JESUS

King Solomon said in Proverbs 16:24: "Pleasant words are like a honeycomb, sweet to the soul and health to the body." Therefore, "God's pleasant words of Holy Scripture" are like a honeycomb for the awesome wellbeing of all born-again believers:

1. God said to His servant Jacob, "Fear not, for I have redeemed you" (Isaiah 43:1, NIV). Likewise, God has redeemed all born-again believers through the precious blood of Jesus Christ, which was shed for us on Calvary's wooden cross; so that we can become Kingdom conscious and live fearlessly and righteously.

2. Therefore, Jesus said to His specially chosen 12 redeemed disciples, (whom He called Apostles): "Fear not, little flock, for it is your Father's good pleasure to give you the Kingdom" (Luke 12:32, KJV).

3. "The Kingdom of God is not a matter of talk, but of power," said St. Paul, in 1 Corinthians 4:30 (NIV): the power of God unto Salvation, which is indeed the power of righteousness, peace and joy in the Holy Spirit, and the power of God through Christ Jesus.

4. "You [the redeemed and righteous] will receive power when the Holy Spirit comes on you," said Jesus, in Acts 1:8 (NIV).

5. And Jesus continued, in Luke 10:19, in the NIV Bible: "Behold, I give you power to tread on serpents and scorpions, and over all the power of the enemy [Satan]; and nothing shall by no means hurt you."

6. For, "God did not give us a spirit of timidity [or fear], but a spirit

of power, of love and self-discipline [or a sound mind, as the KJV Bible has it]." (2 Timothy 1:7, NIV)

7. "Wealth and honor come from you [God]; you are the ruler of all things. In your hands are strength and power to exalt and give strength to all"—especially to the redeemed and the righteous. (1 Chronicles 29:12, NIV)

8. Proverbs 10:22 in the NIV Bible says: "The blessings of the Lord, it maketh rich, and he addeth no sorrow with it." (That is why everyone should rightly covet God's blessings).

9. You must "Seek first his Kingdom and his righteousness, and all these things [blessings] will be given to you as well" (Matthew 6:33, NIV).

10. And, "No weapon forged against you will prevail, and you will refute every tongue that accuses you. This is the heritage of the servants of the Lord, and this is their vindication from me," declares the Lord. (Isaiah 54:17, NIV)

11. So "Do not let your heart be troubled. Trust in God; trust also in me," said Jesus. (John 14:1, NIV).

12. St. Paul says, in Philippians 4:6-7, in the NIV Bible, "Do not be anxious about anything, but in everything, by prayer and petition, with thanksgiving, present your requests to God. And the peace of God which transcends all understanding will guard your hearts and minds in Christ Jesus."

13. Finally, I close with two verses of wisdom from King Solomon's proverbs: Chapter 4, verses 20 and 22, (NIV): "My child, be atten-

tive to my words; incline your ear to my sayings... For they are life to those who find them, and healing to all their flesh."

1

SOME OF SATAN'S PLANS, VS GOD'S PLANS FOR US

1. IN HEAVEN AND IN EDEN

Satan's preoccupation with his negative thoughts, ideas and plans, to overthrow God by usurping His power in heaven, was followed by his [Satan's] prideful and negative confrontation with God and His loyal angelic hosts. That was what really started and predetermined the destiny of Satan and his rebellious cohorts in heaven, God's angelic hosts, and His most valuable creation on earth called man (Adam and Eve). And, during and after Satan's negative, prideful, power confrontation with God in heaven, followed by his instigation of man's disobedience in the Garden of Eden on earth, the word "SIN," coined later on in the Holy Bible as "PRIDE," (or self-worship and a feeling of false greatness), and "REBELLION," (or arrogance and disobedience), was born in Satan and man.

This prideful, arrogant, and rebellious feeling and act of Satan, who was then called "Lucifer," and "The Morning Star"—just like Christ Jesus—before his fall, (because he was so beautiful, radiant and powerful), was followed by God's counter-plan and action to subdue and humble him and his rebellious cohorts from seizing power in heaven, by casting them down to earth and hell.

The book of Luke Chapter10, verse 18, in the Holy Bible, says, "Satan and his rebellious angels fell down from heaven with lightning speed." And this scenario was the origin of King Solomon's many wise biblical sayings about "pride," "arrogance," and "rebellion," in the book of PROVERBS, as well as the Prophet Moses's account of "The Fall of Man," in Genesis Chapter 3.

In the book of Proverbs, King Solomon thus writes, (God speaking through him):

(a) "I hate pride and arrogance, evil behavior and perverse speech" (Proverbs 8:13, NIV).

(b) "When pride comes, then comes disgrace, but with humility comes wisdom [and I add, honor]" (Proverbs 11:2, NIV).

(c) For "Pride only breeds quarrels" (Proverbs 13:10, NIV).

(d) And "Pride goes before destruction, a haughty spirit before a fall" (Proverbs 16:18, NIV).

(e) Therefore, "A man's pride brings him low," says Proverbs 29:23, in the NIV Bible.

And that is what happened to Satan and his rebellious angels in heaven, and Adam and Eve who were then immortals in the Garden of Eden, before their fall (Genesis Chapter 3). Pride and arrogance blinded both parties, and they could not think straight; so they both rebelled against or disobeyed God, and suffered dire consequences.

Then, when Satan received the penalty for his crime and realized the severity of his fall, he jealously began to compare his diminished state of power on earth as a fallen angel, with man's power, before man lost God's favor in the Garden of Eden. Satan felt that God had given immortal man too much power and favor than him; and so, he engineered a plan for man's fall (Genesis 3). For initially, God had made man in His own image and likeness: like a God, though not equal to Him in power, but with absolute power for dominion over the whole earth and all its creatures etc. (Genesis 1:27-28). Consequently, envy, jealousy, covetousness, malice and hatred, crept into Satan's heart and mind; so he felt insulted, belittled, and totally rejected by God. It was then he devised a clandestine, evil, and subtle plan with lies and deception, to dethrone and discredit man, by attacking and subduing Eve (man's weaker vessel). This was his only hope (he believed), to get back at God and man for his demise. So he began by saying to Eve in the Garden of Eden, "Did God really say, 'You must not eat from any tree in the Garden of Eden'?" (Genesis 3:1, NIV).

Eve's reply to Satan, who was then disguised as a talking-serpent and she did not recognize who it was, was, "We may eat fruit from the trees in the garden, but God did say, 'You must not eat from the tree that is in the middle of the garden, and you must not touch it, or, you will die' " (Genesis 3:2-3, NIV).

Then Satan finally said to Eve, to complete his final secret and persuasive plan of deception, "You will not surely die... For God knows that when you eat of it your eyes will be opened, and you will be like God, knowing good and evil" (Genesis 3:4-5, NIV).

Satan really blew Eve's mind! The Holy Bible says, in Genesis 3:6-7 of the NIV Bible:

"When the woman [Eve] saw that the fruit of the tree was good for food and pleasing to the eye, and also desirable for gaining wisdom, she took some and ate it. She also took some and gave to her husband, who was with her, and he ate it. Then the eyes of both of them were opened, and they realized that they were naked; so they sewed fig leaves together, and made covering for themselves."

Note well: All Satan's plans had fallen into place perfectly! Man lost God's special favors and became accursed (Genesis 3:16-19). He was no longer immortal, and he became weak, sinful, and very vulnerable to all kinds of diseases.

2. AFTER EDEN ON EARTH–
SATAN'S STRATEGIES VS GOD'S STRATEGIES

As soon as man (Adam) sinned (or disobeyed God) in the Garden of Eden, God cursed him and his wife (Eve), and the serpent (Satan), for their alliance. And then God banished Adam and Eve from the Garden of Eden.

As a result, today there are basically two kinds of people on this earth—Satan's disciples, and God's blood-washed disciples through Christ Jesus. Those who are trapped by sin and its consequences (or who are still under God's generational curse), and those who live by and under "God's grace and mercy," and have been set free from the generational curse on Adam and Eve, by the power of the precious blood of Jesus Christ shed on Calvary's wooden cross for all repentant sinners. So God's disciples who live under His grace and mercy and the power of Jesus Christ's shed blood, are referred to as "the redeemed and righteous," or "blood washed sinners," called "Saints," who no longer have and enjoy fellowship with Satan, because they have stopped practicing sin (or rebellion). Through their first and continual daily repentance from sin, and their daily profession of faith in Jesus Christ, they have been "justified"* by God.

But be very mindful still today of Satan's schemes; for he is always trying to get many more prideful, arrogant, and rebellious souls than those he already has on his side; so that he and all his rebellious fallen angels (or demons) and earthly disciples, will not stand alone before the judgment seat of Christ on "Judgment Day."* Satan still believes that having a great number of guilty souls to support his cause will force God to lighten his already designated punishment at the end of time. But he is very mistaken; for "Judgment Day" will not be like a classroom-punishment experience, where and when you can "pass the buck."* Apart from Jesus Christ's punishment on him and God's judgment on all "condemned sinners,"* the Saints (or the spiritually oppressed, redeemed and righteous souls) will judge the world.

1 Corinthians 6:2, in the NIV Bible, says, "Do you not know that the Saints will judge the world?"

And despite Satan's persistent deceptions and attempts to distract, oppress, and destroy man in this world, it is also very comforting for us to remember however, that God never intended or intends to leave us comfortless (Joshua 1:5).

Being "omnipotent"* and "omniscient,"* and intently and intensely loving, God already knew about men's ways and had "a back-up plan"* for fallen man's "redemption,"* even before man fell from grace and favor in the Garden of Eden. And never mind God's tardiness sometimes in fulfilling His promises; His ways are not like men's ways, and He always keeps His promises. He is not limited by time or eternity, and His ways are past finding out. If we could understand God—who He is and what He is doing—he would not be God but a man like you and me.

So 2 Peter 3:9 says, "The Lord is not slow in keeping his promise, as some understand slowness. He is patient with you [us], not wanting anyone to perish, but everyone to come to repentance."

So Luke 13:3, in the NIV Bible, says, "Unless you [all of us] repent, you [we] will all perish."

God knows that we are weak and can't survive every trial and test of Satan without His grace and mercy, and the strength and peace of Christ in our lives (Philippians 4:13); and that we are only dust and ashes in His sight (Genesis 2:7; Psalm 103:4); so, most times, He does not punish us for our sins as we deserve (Psalm 103:10). As a result of this situation, Psalm 136:1 says about Him, "His mercy endures forever." And, "As far as the east is from the west, so far does he remove our 'transgressions'* from us" (Psalm 103:12, NIV).

Exodus 34:6, in the NIV Bible, says, "The Lord, the Lord, the compassionate and gracious God, slow to anger,   abounding in love and faithfulness, maintaining love to thousands, and forgiving wickedness, rebellion and sin... Yet he does not leave the guilty unpunished; he punishes the children and their children for the sin of the fathers to the third and fourth generation"--as a result of the generational curse which began with Adam and Eve's sin.

Therefore, God's back-up plan for man's salvation, through Jesus Christ's shed precious blood on Calvary's wooden cross, was properly planned, with much deliberation. It was so perfectly planned, that not even Satan himself could cypher its details with all his problem solving skills.

Satan never believed that Our Savior (Jesus Christ) could and would come into this sinful world, through and as a normal mortal, or human birth, and be conceived by the power of the Holy Spirit. And that God had already chosen and prepared a special and par-ticular virgin for His Son's birth: a virgin called Mary, betrothed to a carpenter called Joseph, from Nazareth.

So the Holy Scripture says in Galatians 4:4, of the NIV Bible, "But when the time had fully come, God sent his Son, born of a woman, born under the law [of the Ten Commandments], to re-deem those under the law [of the generational law curse of Adam and Eve's sin], that we, [the redeemed through Christ Jesus], may receive the full right of Sons [of God]."

Man's "redemption"* for his "salvation"* and "eternal life,"* had to be done partly through natural, physical means, because Adam and Eve were our first, natural, physical parents, who caused all humanity to be condemned for their physical sin of dis-obedience. Therefore, God sent Jesus Christ down from heaven to earth in human form—in a seemingly natural, physical way, as a Godly substitute—"to atone"* for humanity's sin. This means also, that Jesus Christ came into this world to break "the genera-tional-curse cycle"* of human punishment of suffering, death, and hell-fire, for Adam and Eve's sin of disobedience.

Therefore, in reference to man's redemption, Romans 6:23 says, "For the wages of sin is death; [both physical and spiritual], but the gift of God is eternal life in Christ Jesus Our Lord."

Adam and Eve sinned, and so, as we are also spiritual and physical inheritors of the punishment for the crime which they committed, we were all destined to die physically and spiritually like them. But, thanks to Christ Jesus, we are redeemed by his pre-cious blood which He shed for us on Calvary's cross, when He took our place and suffered the punishment we deserve for our sins: this was God's back-up plan for us sinners, so that all of us would not be condemned and perish in hell-fire.

1 Corinthians 15:22, in the NIV Bible, says, "For as in Adam all die, so in Christ all will be made alive."

And John 3:16, in the NIV Bible, says, "For God so loved the world that he gave his one and only Son, that whoever believes in him shall not perish but have eternal life."

This above last quotation is God's basic and final plan and promise for our redemption and salvation, to inherit the coveted prize of eternal life from Him, which Adam and Eve forfeited in the Garden of Eden. So that eventually, all of Holy Scripture pro-ceeded sequentially onwards, from man's first sinful experience in the Garden of Eden, (from Genesis 2:9, 2:16-17, 3:7, and 3:22), followed by John 3:16, when Jesus finally came to redeem human-ity.

Whatever race, color, creed, class, religion, nation, or country you belong to, God's promise for your redemption has and will always remain true and the same, through your faith in Christ Jesus—as long as you believe in your heart, accept, and profess or confess with your mouth that Jesus Christ is "your Lord and personal Savior."*

But remember: Satan has also devised a counter-plan to try to nullify God's redemption plan for all humanity, after his Eden experience with man and God. He never stops working at it, and he never wishes to give it up. His plan is not only to destroy God's people, (the redeemed and the righteous), but also those who blindly and carelessly follow him.

In John 10:10 of the NIV Bible, Jesus says, "The thief [Satan] comes only to steal, kill, and destroy. I have come that they [the redeemed and the righteous] may have life, and have it to the full."

Let us now investigate some of Satan's strategies for stealing, killing, and destroying unbelievers and believers in Christ Jesus, through the power of sin. I hope that my scanty bits of information and wisdom will educate, enrich, protect, stimulate, encourage, and direct the minds and hearts of some careless believers and unbelievers. My experience with Satan may not always be the same as yours or another's, but our saving experience through the power of Christ Jesus, when we believed in our heart and confessed Him with our mouth as our Lord and Personal Savior was the same. Therefore, the very instant that we believed in our heart and confessed Him with our mouth we became "saved."*

Consequently, I have decided to try my best to give you a partly detailed account of God's saving grace and mercy experience through Christ Jesus, in relation to Satan's formidable opposition. Every redeemed, born-again baptized believer knows his own saving experience, and should be able to identify himself with a particular cap of Satan's strategies which fitted or now fits him, as I discuss some of SATAN'S STRATEGIES, VERSUS GOD'S STRATEGIES. I therefore proceed as follows:

2a. WHO AND WHAT DOES SATAN USE?
2b. WHY DOES SATAN USE THEM?
2c. WHERE DOES SATAN USE THEM?
2d. WHEN DOES SATAN USE THEM?
2e. HOW DOES SATAN USE THEM?

Before I answer the above questions, let me warn and remind you (as one born-again, redeemed, righteous, and baptized believer to another), about an important "spiritual truth issue," concerning Satan and his destructive worldly strategies.

You must not think of the power of Satan over you, but the power of Christ Jesus within you and of God's saving grace and mercy—by the redeeming, saving, healing, cleansing, and protection-power of the blood of Jesus Christ, which was shed for us at Calvary; and His powerful and immortal, resurrection experience: meaning that Jesus has already paid the price for our deliverance from Satan and sin's deadly decree. So that our fear of the power of sin to kill and destroy us, through sickness and suffering, and our fear of death, hell, sickness, and the grave, should be no more. You must also remember that Jesus' Godly powers were re-activated, when God raised Him up after three days in the tomb. Therefore, "Greater is he [Jesus] that is in you [or me], than he [Satan] that is in the world." And now, Jesus is sitting at the right hand of God's heavenly throne, interceding and pleading with God for us about our every request. He is Lord, Ruler, King, and Master of Satan and of our lives. And He is alive and well!

Isaiah 53:4-5, in the NIV Bible, says, "Surely, he took up our infirmities, [or our sin, diseases, etc.], and carried our sorrows, yet we considered him stricken by God, smitten by him and afflicted; the punishment that brought us peace was upon him, and by his wounds we are healed."

This also means that Satan is now a defeated foe, because death, sickness, hell, and the grave, could not hold Jesus down as captive, or defeat Him. Jesus arose triumphantly on Easter morning with an immortal and glorified body, powerful, healthy, and strong. And that same resurrection power, (God's power) which quickened or gave "new life"* and power to His mortal dead body, to free Him and us from Adam and Eve's generational curse and Satan's power, is still available to all repentant sinners today. Therefore, don't fear Satan's destructive decree to steal, kill, and destroy your life, or your well-being and joy; "For the joy of the Lord is our strength," says Nehemiah 8:10.

Unless God gives Satan permission to afflict you or test your faith, as He allowed in Job's case in the book of Job in the Holy Bible, Satan will have no power over you. And as long as you remain in "Jesus Christ's Safety-Fence,"* you will have all the power, protection, faith, joy, healing, and the provision that you need to overcome Satan and his demonic disciples, because you are a redeemed or righteous human soul on fire for God.

Now, let me deal with the previous topics of 2a to 2e: SATAN'S STRATEGIES VS GOD'S.

2a. WHO AND WHAT DOES SATAN USE?

Satan uses the subtle, deceptive, influential, tantalizing, and compelling psychological power of his "demon possessed people"* and "demons,"* and other sinister spiritually and physically addictive and deceptive agents, to subdue, control, and destroy, all his vulnerable hosts. And remember again, his main aim is to destroy especially, all the redeemed and righteous human souls on fire for God, because God has a special love for them.

He also subtly and deceptively uses the diverse physical, negative, direct and indirect influences of corrupt social media, as his main weapon of mass-destruction for our minds, souls, and bodies; for he knows that what the eye perceives, or the mind can conceive or imagine, the body will usually crave for and try to possess and/or enjoy, because the mind especially, is a tremendously powerful force and agent, consciously, with faith in God or Satan. And the body will or may eventually and finally follow the mind's lead or directives.

Satan uses social media technology like television, radio, computer, cell phone, I-phone, I-pad, tablet, video game, cd, cassette, disc, jump drive (or thumb drive), and other agents, like corrupt graphic arts exhibiting nudity and obscenity in pictures, sketches, and paintings, and in the newspapers. Nudist magazines and other corrupt sexual devices like dildos, etc., in porn shops, also play a major role in generating financial returns in Satan's corrupt sexual trade; as well as writings of graffiti on walls. Satan also uses pornography in peep-shows, brothels, X-rated cinema movies, night clubs (strip-tease), discos, casinos, etc. etc.–most of them depicting and promoting sexual promiscuity, and violent shooting and stabbing crimes, with alcohol and/or, illegal drug-abuse, gambling, witchcraft, human sex trafficking, money laundering, blackmail, and occult activity. Now note well: don't fool yourself, both the righteous and the unrighteous are targeted, and they both occasionally or finally become victims of Satan's clandestine schemes.

Consequently, corrupt social media attacks man's mind, soul, body, and spirit, with the archenemy particularly trying to possess and destroy man's mind, and ultimately his soul–especially the minds and souls of those who are weak in faith, hope, and love, in and for Almighty God. As a result, Satan's agents, (the possessed people and demons), try to influence all vulnerable hosts to believe, that God's promises for "abundant life" on earth and "eternal life" in the hereafter, for the redeemed and the righteous, through Christ Jesus, are just myths. When I talk about "abundant life" on earth, I refer to our coveted prizes for prosperity: like health, wealth, godly protection, and a spirit of love, peace, joy, forgiveness, self-control, wisdom, understanding, patience, etc.— "a new life" or "regeneration," through faith in Jesus Christ and the Holy Spirit, and our hope and faith in Almighty God. Furthermore, as regards "eternal life" in the hereafter as part of "God's abundant life package," I refer to a life of endless bliss: unending joy, praise, worship, peace, and no more sickness or pain and sadness in heaven. But Satan's agents are always trying their best to influence people to believe otherwise by deception, that a life of lawlessness is the best way to go; and this is a lie from the pit of hell! For Satan is a liar, a thief, and an accuser of the brethren on earth, and to God in heaven. All that he wants is to steal their peace and joy—their joy and peace of salvation on earth, and God's promise and reward of joyful and eternal bliss in heaven.

Whoever falls for or believes Satan's lies, illusions, temptations, and deceptions, will eventually and finally become a victim of his mind-games for physical and mental afflictions, and will finally die—spiritually and physically.

Satan occasionally and deceptively afflicts and plagues both believers and unbelievers with mind-games: like lust, malice, pride, jealousy, envy, hatred, greed, covetousness, fear, guilt, worry, anxiety, depression, tension, paranoia, slothfulness, doubt, suicidal thoughts, discouragement, unbelief and disbelief in God and their fellowmen, low self-esteem, despair, unpleasant memories of the past, (especially their failures and disappointments), persecution complexes, addiction denial, and sometimes false high self-esteem (or pride), just like himself when he was in heaven—which finally leads to arrogance and rebellion against God, man, and the social norms, and finally, self-destruction.

Like fallen man in the Garden of Eden, a rebellious or an addicted soul who has become possessed and afflicted by Satan and his mind-games (or schemes), will occasionally or finally look to or for someone or some situation to blame for his/her condition, when he is or becomes desperate. Consequently, he now needs help: spiritual counselling and redemption through Christ Jesus, or psychiatric help or both helps, with the intercessory prayers of the saints, working together to restore his body, mind, soul, and spirit, to complete wellness.

That is when and where Jesus Christ should come into the picture as "the great physician," and the physician of all physicians. He can restore any fallen man completely—physically, intellectually, and spiritually, with no side effects. He is completely able and capable. He has and is still healing all kinds of diseases today, through the anointed and supernatural ability of His humble and faithful, faith-filled disciples, and many God-gifted physicians who have humble faith in him.

There is no yoke of affliction inflicted by Satan and his disciples, or natural man, that Jesus Christ has not broken or healed—all afflictions of body, mind, soul, and spirit, and especially of spiritual wickedness in high places (Matthew 8:14-17). Just imagine, one anointed man of God (Jesus Christ) did it all! And He has given to some of His anointed disciples, apostles, and Holy Spirit-filled believers, the same powers and authority that Almighty God gave Him—when He walked on earth as "the greatest physician"—to evangelize and completely restore fallen man (Mark 16:15-18).

In Matthew 28:18-20, Jesus said to His chosen disciples, who were redeemed and righteous believers, "All authority [or power] in heaven and on earth has been given to me. Therefore go and make disciples of all nations … And surely I am with you always, to the very end of the age."

And in Mark 16:17-18, Jesus also said about His faith-filled and anointed apostles and disciples, when commissioning them: "In my name they [or you] will drive out demons; they [and you] will speak in new tongues; they [and you] will pick up snakes with their [or your] hands; and when they [or you] drink deadly poison, it will not hurt them [or you] at all; they [or you] will place their hands on sick people, and they [the persons] will get well."

So whereas in the physical realm medical doctors can cure some diseases, Jesus' disciples are different; they can heal or cure all kinds of diseases through their faith in the mighty name and power of Jesus Christ—even diseases of spiritual wickedness in high places which baffle physical doctors. God has given them the authority and power to do so, through "Jesus Christ's Great Commission" in Mark 16:17-18.

That is why St. Paul says in Ephesians 6:10, in the NIV Bible, to all the redeemed and righteous, born-again, baptized believers,

> "Finally, be strong in the Lord, and in his mighty power. Put on the full armor of God, so that you can take your stand against the devil's schemes. For our struggle is not against flesh and blood, but against the rulers, against the authorities, against the powers of this dark world and against the spiritual forces of evil in the heavenly realm."

Please read also Ephesians 6:13-18 carefully, about how you could use "the full armor of God" to protect yourself against Satan's schemes.

Now let me inform you that as a believer, you should not fear natural man—even though Satan endows him with the spiritual gifts of the evil forces of darkness in the heavenly realm, and he has become possessed. You should only watch out and guard yourself against his powers and capability for wickedness and destruction, by putting on "the full armor of God" (Ephesians 6:13-18). And then affirm and demonstrate your faith with power, "in the powerful and mighty Name and Blood of Jesus," as His resurrected immortal power within you, and as a redeemed and righteous human soul on fire for God, to subdue and destroy him.

Remember again what Ephesians 6:10 says, "Be strong in the Lord [Jesus] and in his mighty power": (The immortal power of

Jesus Christ's resurrected and anointed body and spirit, which conquered Satan, our fear of death, hell, all evil, sickness, and the grave); so that "No weapon forged against you will prevail" (Isaiah 54:17).

2b. WHY DOES SATAN USE THEM?

Satan uses his demons, demon-possessed-people, animals and things, as his agents of destruction, because they make his deceptive work easier.

His uses them through his power of self-transformation, lies, deception, and camouflage, so that his prey, host, or victims, will not recognize him and his strategies or schemes—just as he did to Eve in the Garden of Eden, and she did not recognize him as the talking serpent (Genesis 3).

For example: when searching for your compatible spouse, (Miss or Mister right), you may encounter a very beautiful woman or a very handsome man, and either one may be an unknown death sentence or a trap for you—because they might or may have a deadly contagious disease which he or she might be hiding. And this can be one of Satan's tricks to destroy you. Remember what the Holy Bible says: Satan can appear or transform himself as "an angel of light"* (2 Corinthians 11:14). He will make sure that this woman or man he presents to you looks very healthy, stunningly attractive and very beautiful, or handsome, and very appealing or desirable; so that you or the opposite sex will say things and act in a manner that is abnormal and tantalising. Consequently, your lust (or negative emotions) will be aroused, and you may get out of control (or do and say stupid and crazy things). For, not many people can control their lusts and other negative emotions when Satan is at work on them. Satan is an unmatched, super-incredible grandmaster at using and presenting diverse temptations, deceptions, and seductions, to everyone. If he does not succeed one way, he usually tries another or more sophisticated approach—meaning that he may even appeal to your intellectual or spiritual pride, or your compassionate emotions. He can satisfy any need or desire that you have, except "the fruit of the Holy Spirit," and "God's peace and joy through Christ Jesus," which surpasses all understanding.

So St. Paul states so rightly in Romans 7:15, 18, and 19, in the GNB, the result of this fore-mentioned scenario, when he says that a person without Christ and the guidance of the Holy Spirit in his or her life is defenseless and very vulnerable to Satan's negative schemes. He admitted that even a strong believer like himself became vulnerable sometimes too. He said, "I do not understand what I do; for I don't do what I would like to do, but instead I do what I hate... For even though the desire to do good is in me, I am not able to do it... I do the evil that I do not want to do."

As an unbeliever, you will always be controlled by your weakest and strongest emotions of lust, when Satan's temptations and other evil desires besiege you; and your mind and body will always be Satan's playground and stronghold, instead of the Holy Spirit's stronghold of self-control. Self-control will always be a major problematic issue of and in your life, and that is what Satan wants and likes.

Self-control may seem to be a very simple issue to you, but look at how it is very complicated and difficult. A wise old Greek philosopher called Aristotle, who lived in 384—322 BC, said about controlling one's anger:

"Anybody can become angry—that is easy, but to become angry with the right person and to the right degree and at the right time, and for the right purpose and in the right way—that is not in everybody's power and is not easy."

Satan, his demons, and possessed people, are very cunning, possessive, territorial, subtle, deceptive, patient, and persistent, and are archenemies of God's redeemed and righteous people. They want to have full control of God's people's minds and souls, but they can't; because the peace of Jesus Christ and the gifts (or fruit) of the Holy Spirit are God's people's answers for deliverance from this problem. So Satan realizes that he is fighting a losing battle here, even though the redeemed and righteous sometimes falter. By God's grace and mercy also, they are always able to "bounce back" through humility and faith in Jesus Christ. Their humility, patience, peace, joy, self-control, wisdom, understanding, compassion, faith, and love of God, always help them to persevere in righteousness.

2c. WHERE DOES SATAN USE THEM?

Satan uses his "demons"* and other "workers of iniquity,"* everywhere that temptation, deception, illusion, and camouflage is possible, effective, and can become a major challenge for us. And just as God is everywhere on earth, Satan and his demons and demon-possessed people are everywhere on earth. They are even where you think you are alone, and think that is a secret hiding-place for you—especially your thoughts. Therefore, there is no place you can hide from him in this world. Your only recourse and hope from him, is to get inside and remain within "Jesus Christ's safety fence,"* as one preacher remarked. He meant that you should always stay at the foot of Calvary's wooden cross, where you will be continually covered, cleansed, healed, protected, and redeemed of all unrighteousness, "by the blood of Jesus," and sustained "by the word of your testimony." There, you will find peace, grace, mercy, protection and rest, to conquer and overcome Satan and his legions. God's Holy Word says in Revelation 12:11, that we can overcome the devil "by the blood of the Lamb and by the word of [our] testimony." And we can do so in righteousness, anywhere that Satan and his executioners confront us: in the work-place, church, on the play-ground, at school, at home (in our domestic life), in the military, political and community organizations, etc. etc.

2d. WHEN DOES SATAN USE THEM?

Satan uses his demons and demon-possessed people to try to corrupt, trap, and destroy all the redeemed and the righteous souls, when their faith in and love for God, and resistance to temptation and corruption is low. So that these targeted souls usually become impatient, intolerant, nervous, desperate, depressed, hopeless, sometimes arrogant, critically negative, and sometimes develop a lack of self-control. These phenomena usually happens when there are individual or personal problems, or strained relations between individuals in marriage, the work-places, churches, schools, etc. etc. for example.

The demons and corrupt persons' eyes and ears are always very sensitive, attuned, and wide open and watchful for signs of weakness and corruption in everyone—especially believers, (or the redeemed and righteous), who are practicing their faith. For, the more the redeemed or righteous believers practice their faith, it is the more or greater and stronger their temptations, trials, and persecutions, will be from Satan.

So when the redeemed and righteous believers are challenged by Satan and his disciples, they should pray continually by calling upon "the name of Jesus," and also plead deliverance through His precious blood shed on Calvary. For there is power in His name, and in His shed precious Blood. His precious blood has the power to free, deliver, protect, cleanse (or wash), and to save anyone who put their trust in Him. Believers should always plead "the Name" and "the Blood" of Jesus in every adverse situation, and ask the Holy Spirit to comfort them. Then they should continue their prayerful defense for protection through their affirmation of faith in God for positive outcome, by reciting prayers for protection like Psalms 27, 91, 121, 23, 18, or 140, etc. etc. Then Satan and his cohorts will fly away. For Satan trembles when he sees the weakest saint on his knees. "The prayer of the righteous is powerful!" (James 5:16, NIV).

Satan and his disciples always come prepared for battle, because they know fully what they are doing when they are attacking believers. Therefore, believers must be very vigilant, very prayerful, very careful, very strong, and exercise their faith in God through Christ Jesus at all times. Believers have also been encouraged by Jesus in Matthew 11:28-30, as well as in 1 Peter 5:7, to cast all their anxieties and burdens (or problems) on Him (Jesus), in faith, and He will take care of their problems, including Satan. All we have to do and say now is "yes!" and "amen" to that!

Now let me digress here a little while, to narrate a little scenario about a few of my experiences with Satan and my co-workers, in some of my workplaces, and how God, through Christ Jesus, worked out every business problem in and through "divine order"* for me.

In some business places that I worked, some owners exploited their employees by underpaying them, making them work hard for long hours without overtime payment rewards, and in sub-standard physical conditions which were conducive to ill health. But, little did both the owners and some workers know, Satan had already set up strongholds in their minds; so that, while the owners and some bosses underpaid their workers, the workers stole the company's goods and money, and the businesses had to operate on a near or borderline state of bankruptcy, and/or overdraft and credits.

In the eyes of God, neither the oppressor nor the oppressed can boast of their sin as a lesser evil than each other; for Satan had both of them destroying each other. I have seen this evil phenomenon repeat itself many times in my 34 years in the business world. But never mind! Despite Satan's plans for accommodating the oppressor and the oppressed, God also has a special plan for all sinners; so there is hope for every thief. The vilest offender who truly believes in Jesus Christ and repents of his sin, can and will be "saved."

Look how loving and merciful God is: "His love [and mercy] endures forever," says Psalm 136:1, in the NIV; and "He does not treat us as our sins deserve or repay us according to our iniquities" (Psalm 103:10, NIV). Therefore, it was not too late for the crucified repentant thief on Calvary's cross, next to our dying Savior, to experience the joy of salvation, and look forward to the joy of eternal life in the hereafter. For, he acknowledged his sin with guilt and perfect contrition (or sorrow) in his heart, and then said to Jesus, "Jesus, remember me when you come into your Kingdom" (Luke 23:42, NIV).

Then Jesus said to him, "I tell you the truth, today you will be with me in paradise" (Luke 23:43, NIV).

Note well: I was overjoyed when a few of my cited workmates gave their lives to Jesus. God loves all sinners, but He hates their practice of sin.

I have known some commercial oppressors who have taken to using alcohol and smoking, to drown their guilty feelings and sorrows, when they exploit their employees and never repented of their sin of theft and oppression. Some of their victims (or the oppressed employees), also resorted to abusing alcohol, or taking or peddling illegal drugs; because they also realized that their salaries could not support their lifestyle or standard of living that they want to maintain in society. So some became "drug barons"* in the illegal drug trade. Others got involved in crime. It is therefore important to note that Satan can deceive anyone's heart and mind with feelings of greed, envy, and covetousness, especially in the case of most misguided, unsuccessful, and under-privileged youth, and some unsuccessful, adults. But when one is blessed with the peace of Christ, and the joy of salvation, he becomes contented with the little or any measure that he has been blessed with by God. And, if there is a need for anything else or more in his or her life, he or she usually work hard, pray, and patiently wait on the Lord for such a desired blessing. And he/she prospers soon enough. I thank God, through Christ Jesus, that this was and still is the path that I travel today; for honesty is the best policy. Praise and bless His holy name!

St. Paul in Philippians 4:19 says about God's redeemed and righteous people, "My God will meet [supply] all your needs according to his glorious riches in Christ Jesus."

So some of the redeemed and righteous believers (including me), trusted God for a break-through and right outcome of blessings in our workplace, and it did materialize in "Divine Order,"* and right timing. Our patience, faith in God, and tolerance of adverse situations with self-control, finally rewarded us. Some of us were promoted with salary increases, and we were able to pay off our loans and mortgages before our designated retirement leave. We thank God for our faith in Him, and positive thinking through Christ Jesus. "Divine Order" surely prevailed and did the trick for us. "Satan lost!"

As for some of the oppressed workers who indulged in alcohol abuse, smoking, and illegal drug taking or peddling it, in the prime of their family-life at work and home, Satan still has some of them reaching out for alcohol and illegal drugs to console themselves. Note well, Satan has left some of them with an occasional craving; and others, with an addiction problem which can't and will never full their inner emptiness for "God's abundant life package"*--which includes the real peace and joy that Jesus gives. Therefore, some of them are not able to work anymore, while others refuse to or don't want to work to become productive in and for society. They therefore hail under the banner of delinquency, and are sometimes a threat or burden to good, upright, and productive citizens. So Satan uses some of them to destabilize or disturb the peaceful and normal functioning of civil society with conforming citizens, while others who are helpless and hopeless cases are put away and cared for in special social institutions.

2e. HOW DOES SATAN USE THEM?

There are incredible and innumerable ways by which and how Satan uses his demons, demon-possessed-people, and other physically destructive and seductive agents, to steal, kill, and destroy, both believers and unbelievers.

The most glaring and destructive agents that Satan used against humanity in early biblical-times, was our first parents (Adam and Eve). Both of them were Satan's agents of mass-destruction for all humanity, by committing their first sin of disobedience (Genesis 3)—with Eve being the main instigator of Satan's selfish, clandestine plan, because she was man's weaker vessel, and the most powerful agent that Satan could use then, to destroy God's plan for humanity.

Believe it or not, Satan had no doubt that when he used his subtle, transforming, demonic, seductive, and deceptive influence on Eve, that she would help him to accomplish his destructive mission. And so, that is how immortal man lost the grace and favor of Almighty God after his creation (Genesis 3:1-13).

Satan forever plays with and capitalizes on man's mind and emotions—especially man's weakness for woman. Genesis 2:23 strongly implies this fact, when the first created man (Adam) received Eve as his soul mate from God. Man became so thrilled and filled with wonder, joy, and amazement—like a little child who received his first Christmas toy—that he exclaimed with joy and contentment before he yielded to Satan's deceptive temptation: "This is now bone of my bones and flesh of my flesh; she shall be called woman, for she was taken out of man [Adam]."

Unlike today, in all the other animals and creatures that Adam named, none of them was his match or a suitable choice and compatible companion. So when God provided a soul mate or suitable companion for him, he gave his beloved companion a "cushy" (or soft, gentle, and loving name), which was highly suggestive of her comforting, consoling, soothing, and very close connection with him—even though she was sometimes mesmerizing and domineering. Consequently, man's greatest temptation before, and sometimes today, came and still comes from Satan's use of many beautiful, tantalizing, deceptive, charming, and sexy women, or handsome men, who are very wise in the art of seduction and deception like himself.

But today, man's greatest temptation from Satan has been taken over or replaced by Satan's use of a deadlier weapon called illegal drugs—a new-age, super-deadly temptation of mass-destruction for humanity. And so today, Satan's disciples risk their precious lives to secure a slice in this illegal drug trade, which uses demonic deception to destroy naive men and women, and at the same time provides affluence for parasitic men called drug barons, who are able to afford almost everything they desire, including plenty of women, from it.

Satan is such a cunning foe, that when he and his disciples promote the illegal drug trade, they do so in such a way that they successfully impress the confused, misguided, deceived, desperate, and fallen youth especially. They try their best to create an impression "that all is well and easy going," with those who consume illegal drugs, and those who do drug-trafficking. Satan and his worldly followers never present or show the real statistics of the many casualties in the illegal drug trade. All that they show is the rich and extravagant life-style of the drug-lords—such as the possession of many big houses, yachts, vehicles, aircraft, jewels, expensive clothes, many acres of land, security dogs, house servants, security guards and overflowing bank accounts. They are also portrayed as persons who are feared in the community, because they have influence with high-ranking law enforcement officers, and many other corrupt social elite—while honest little you and I are working very hard and patiently to achieve.

So while Satan, his demons, and his other worldly disciples (or demon-possessed-persons) are having a very nice time seducing and destroying the innocent and naïve youth with illegal drugs, some adults who are weak willed, and some other persons who are already addicted and/or possessed, become hooked for lifetime.

Rest assured, when Satan uses his demon-possessed-persons and other social elite, he does not only make sure that they are corrupt and greedy, but also matchlessly powerful, influential, and unlimited in their knowledge and skills of "money laundering."* For affluence and power, most times, are the criteria, source, and mother of all corruption, with diabolic influences. That is why some law enforcement officers and many influential elite find themselves on "Satan's pay-roll."* Their love and greed for money and other corruption, like illegal-drug-peddling, gambling, male and female prostitution, child-pornography, and money-laundering etc. is like a cancer within them, slowly destroying them from within, before manifesting itself externally. And many persons— even including some who claim to be righteous or religious—find it difficult to resist such a honey-decked, lustful, and challenging temptation from Satan.

Then slowly but surely, and finally, as in most affluent and corrupt countries like Sodom and Gomorrah of biblical times (in Genesis 3), the confused same sex, or homosexual tendency issue usually becomes "a norm,"* and Satan and his disciples instigate both genders to solicit and seduce one or both sexes among young and older persons. And sometimes, not even their manner of dressing may suggest or help you to identify who is straight and who is gay; for some of them are as deceptive as Satan himself. And because Satan has influenced both sexes to go so very far with their sinister and corrupt behavior, they have also denied and publicly opposed God's biblical plans for marriage between male and female.

As a result, some of each gender has become totally supportive of and participative in same-sex marriage, and they have no feelings of guilt or shame about it. This situation is still being promoted and supported today, because Satan has strategically placed and uses his agents of corruption in many influential and prominent positions of modern society—like in religious circles (among both laity and clergy), in the political arena, in schools, hotels, the military, the police force, hospitals, and the commercial sector, etc.. And there are little or no stigmas against such persons, except in some parts of the Middle East, like Iran and Iraq, where the punishment for such behavior is death.

Despite all the sexual or gender-related seduction, confusion, and deception caused by Satan and his disciples in family and community life today, there is still a new-age, super-deadly and immediately addictive illegal drug called "fentanyl," that Satan and his disciples use to destroy all vulnerable humanity. It is so deadly, that there is no other illegal drug that has claimed more lives in the world.

This illegal, super-addictive, deadly drug is so powerful, that it surpasses all the other first-time drug use samples in their suicidal mortality rate. This is how Satan and his disciples urgently try their best to destroy and annihilate humanity's well-being, at every second the clock ticks.

Therefore, we have to be very careful at all times wherever we go. For I have heard that some persons, (Satanic disciples especially, and some other persons who may also pose as a close friend), may maliciously and sometimes jokingly put this illegal substance into food or beverages for you or others. And you can rest assured that they do so because Satan and his well-trained crew have already taught them exactly how to introduce and market all illegal drugs to problematic and/or addicted persons.

Let me introduce here, my little humble and superficial speculation about Adam and Eve's rebellious attitude against God in the Garden of Eden, as regards when they ate the forbidden fruit then, which can also represent the illegal drugs today, or any forbidden activity that we should not indulge ourselves in.

Have you ever wondered what would happen to man from creation, if he was not so inquisitive, careless, and rebellious, by eating the forbidden fruit in the Garden of Eden? Maybe Adam and Eve would still be immortal today! I say so, because God gave each of them a free will to choose between life and death, and they chose death. It was their sin of disobedience or wrong choice, (including Eve's curiosity), that destroyed their cordial relationship, including their immortality and favor with Almighty God. So, as the old English saying goes, whether it is for a forbidden fruit or taking illegal drugs, etc., "curiosity killed the cat!" And it will still kill the cat today! Humanity has suffered much in the past for this bad choice, and they are still paying a deadly price for this same mistake today: nothing has changed!

On second thought also, while man was sinless and immortal in the Garden of Eden, maybe God would have found or designed a legitimate plan or way for Adam and Eve to replenish the earth with sinless offspring, if they had made the right choice—just as God did for Mary and Joseph for Jesus' birth. For "With God all things are possible." So that eventually, all God's creation would live in peace, harmony, love, joy, happiness and health forever.

But who am I to question God's plans? His ways are past finding out, and as another English saying goes: "Of what good sense it is to cry over already spilled milk?" The wrong has already been done and God has already sent Jesus on earth to pay the price for its consequences. Therefore, there is no need to worry any more but to work out our own salvation with fear and trembling, as St. Paul said in Philippians 2:12.

Every time people (or humanity) disobey God's laws for righteous living, Satan and his agents quickly step into the picture to have them hooked, addicted, or possessed, sinfully. The Holy Bible speaks clearly and explicitly, in Proverbs 1:22, about humanity's carelessness, which caused and still causes Satan to have and maintain strongholds in our lives.

Proverbs 1:22, in the NIV Bible, says, "For the waywardness of the sinful will kill him, and the complacency of the fools will destroy them."

With man's subjective waywardness because of his evil carnal desires and Satan's influence, and God's generational curse for our rebellious attitude, Satan ceaselessly bombards man's mind with corrupt worldly thoughts of lies, temptation, and deception, to trap him. And most of the time Satan does this work through a medium or agent: an animal, thing, or person, like when he deceived Eve in the Garden of Eden, in Genesis 3.

So just be mindful and very careful about Satan's schemes and favors, especially those involving your self-gratification through the lust of the eyes and of the flesh.

Ninety-nine percent of Satan's schemes for humanity's destruction are done by addicted persons who are possessed, and they support and promote corrupt visual and audio social media— especially because they are fully aware and convinced of what corrupt social media can do to destroy man's mind, body, soul, and spirit, through God's precious gift of sight and hearing.

Holy Scriptures say in the NIV Bible, "The eyes are the lamp of the body. If your eyes are good [healthy], the whole body will be full of light [looking radiant]. But if your eyes are bad, your whole body will be full of darkness [sickly]" (Matthew 6:22-23, NIV).

So be careful what you see, or watch and listen to.

Note well: amongst our five senses (seeing, hearing, tasting, feeling and smelling), God's gift of sight and hearing can have the most disastrous effects and long-lasting consequences on and in a person's mind. That is why Satan wants to control man's mind.

If Satan and his agents try to trap you through the lust of the eyes and of the flesh, just remember who you are through Christ Jesus.

You are a transformed, righteous, redeemed, born-again, and baptized believer through and in Christ Jesus, and God has a special plan for your life. You must therefore claim your spiritual and physical inheritance of deliverance, freedom, and victory through Christ Jesus. How? You must first rebuke and resist Satan and call him a liar, because he has always been and still is the accuser of "the brethren,"* before God and man. And he continually tries to steal their joy. Then, prayerfully call upon the Holy Spirit and Jesus to take full control of your mind, body, and spirit, so that all the corrupt thoughts and feelings within you will be held captive by them, and will be replaced by righteous or spiritual thoughts of "Truth" alone. Satan and his demons, and his possessed people, will then flee from you (James 4:7). And eventually, you will be able to claim your Holy Spirit inheritance of all the positive spiritual gifts of Galatians 5:22-23, especially self-control, patience, peace, wisdom, joy, humility, and your faith in God through Christ Jesus, which is of paramount importance in such times of trials and temptations. Then you will experience the deliverance, peace, joy, and freedom that God gives to all the redeemed and righteous believers in Christ Jesus, and the Holy Spirit's wise counsel and comfort.

St. Paul therefore reminds us in Romans 8:1-2, in the NIV Bible, "Therefore, there is now no condemnation for those who are in Christ Jesus, because through Christ Jesus the law of the Spirit of life set [us] free from the law of sin and death."

Satan can try all his schemes, and he will not succeed completely against God's anointed, redeemed and righteous people; for they will always "bounce back"* if they fall or fail. For "We are more than conquerors," says St. Paul in Romans 8:37, in the NIV Bible. And, "If God is for us, who can be against us?" (Romans 8:31, NIV).

In Romans 8:36-38, NIV, St. Paul therefore concludes, "For I am convinced that neither death nor life, neither angels nor demons, neither the present nor the future, nor any powers, neither height nor depth, nor anything else in all creation, will be able to separate us from the love of God that is in Christ Jesus our Lord."

Satan cannot harm you unless God allows him to do so. Just remember what God says in Matthew 10:29-31, in the NIV Bible: "Are not two sparrows sold for a penny? Yet not one of them will fall to the ground apart from the will of the Father. And even the hairs of your head are all numbered. So don't be afraid; you are worth more than many sparrows."

You must also remember that you are "a child of God,"* and "a redeemed human soul on fire for Him." So a little or great temporary affliction from Satan will not harm or kill you; for God is always in control. And most times, every trial and temptation that you face is only to strengthen you and increase your faith in God, every time you experience simple or greater deliverance. You should also remember here, God's servant called Job, in the Holy Bible. After his afflictions and trials, he received twice as much or even greater rewards and blessings, than he had before God allowed Satan to afflict and tempt him. He passed God's test (Job 42:10-17).

The more you endure and persevere in your trials and temptations, it is the greater your testimonies and rewards will be after each of your deliverances; for both God and Jesus Christ have promised not to leave us comfortless (Joshua 1:5; John 14:18). King David, a man after God's own heart and a great man of prayer, attests to this phenomenon in Psalm 34:19-20 (NIV). He said, "The good man suffers many troubles, but the Lord saves him from them all; ... The Lord preserves him completely ...."

God is always preparing the good human souls (or the righteous and the redeemed) for extraordinary service and blessings on earth, in His Kingdom ministry; while Satan is always preparing his demon-possessed-persons and demons for evil deeds alone. And whereas God's plans are to prepare His disciples to build a better world and to reach out for the coveted gifts of peace and prosperity on earth, and eternal life in the hereafter, Satan's plans are to invent, promote, support, construct, and introduce, all evil schemes, tricks, and devices of corruption and mass-destruction, to annihilate all God's people. This is a battle that will never end until Jesus Christ comes again in glory on earth, as "The Great Judge and King" on God's throne, to judge all creation: all the living and the dead, including Satan and all his demons and possessed persons, who practice spiritual wickedness in high places.

"May Jesus Christ be praised, and to God be the glory!"

2

GOD'S CALL AND OUR MISSION

God's call and our mission, as regards His choices of believers for special anointing of power, protection, and authority, to do His Kingdom ministry on earth, can best be understood by reading the Holy Bible's featured accounts of His calls and charges, of the prophet Samuel in the book of 1 Samuel, the prophet Jeremiah, in the book of Jeremiah, Jesus Christ's call of His first disciples, (Peter and Andrew), in Matthew 4:19, and the account of Paul of Tarsus, (the converted criminal who became one of the greatest Christian saints), in the book of Acts—as well as many other past and present day converts like myself. Some were called and chosen for ministry from childhood, like the prophet Samuel in 1 Samuel chapter 3; while others like the prophet Jeremiah, were called and chosen from their mother's womb (Jeremiah 20:9), and some as teens and older.

But notwithstanding, the most appropriate and explicit information about God's call and our mission was given by Jesus Christ himself, when He addressed His 12 disciples (called apostles), in Matthew 4:19 and 28:18-20; John 15:16; Luke 10:19-20; Mark

16:15-16; John 16:33 and 15:17; and St. Paul, in Galatians 6:2, and 2 Timothy 2:3, respectively, in the NIV Bible.

Jesus Christ said: "Come, follow me... and I will make you fishers of men" (Matthew 4:19, NIV).

And for Our mission: "All authority in heaven and on earth has been given to me. Therefore, go and make disciples of all nations... and teaching them to obey everything I have commanded you. And surely I am with you always, to the very end of the age" (Matthew 28:18-20).

"You did not choose me, [said Jesus], but I chose you and appointed you to go and bear fruit—fruit that will last" (John 15:16, NIV).

"I have given you authority to trample on snakes and scorpions and to overcome all the power of the enemy; nothing will harm you. However, do not rejoice that the spirits [demons] submit to you, but rejoice that your names are written in heaven" (Luke 10:19, NIV).

"Go into the world and preach the Good News to all creation. Whoever believes and is baptized will be saved, but whoever does not believe will be condemned" (Mark 16:15-16, NIV).

"In this world you will have trouble. But take heart! I have overcome the world"—which means, we too can overcome it (John 16:33, NIV).

So "Love each other" (John 15:17, NIV).

Therefore St. Paul said to the Galatians in Galatians 6:2: "Help carry one another's burdens." And to Timothy, (a young convert), in 2 Timothy 2:3: "Endure hardship... like a good soldier of Christ Jesus." "For God gets His best soldiers from the highlands of affliction," says one of my daily meditation issues of "Our Daily Bread."

St. Paul also emphatically states in Holy Scripture, that we must owe no man nothing but love; for apart from faith in God, love is the key to righteous living.

Love is such a valuable asset of our Christian life, that the apostle John repeatedly emphasized it in his gospel and epistle messages. Had it not been for God's love for sinful humanity, after Adam and Eve disobeyed Him, He would not have sent His Son (Jesus Christ) to redeem us from sin on Calvary's wooden cross. And so, we would still be condemned to die in hell-fire for our sins, according to Romans 6:23. Without Jesus Christ's expressed sacrificial love by His death on Calvary's cross for us, we would not have had salvation (or be saved)—so that our love for God and faith in Jesus Christ could achieve the impossible. And although it is impossible to please God without faith, God also shows us that real or genuine spiritual love is so very important and invaluable (1 Corinthians 13:4-7), that it is and always has to be the intrinsic and basic motive of our Christian life. For it precedes and outlives our faith and hope in God, and many other virtues of our Christian life experiences, when serving God. That is why St. Paul says in 1 Corinthians 13:8, GNB, "Love is eternal;" and in 1 Corinthians 13: 7, GNB, "Love never gives up, and its faith, hope, and patience never fail." Therefore 1 Corinthians 13:1-3 and verse 13 says,

> "If I speak in the tongues of men and of angels, but have not love, I am a resounding gong, or a clanging cymbal. If I have the gift of prophesy and can fathom all mysteries and all knowledge, and if I have a faith that can move mountains, but have not love, I am nothing. If I give all I possess to the poor and surrender my body to the flames, but have not love, I gain nothing… And now these three remain: faith, hope, and love, but the greatest of these is love."

So if you are in Christ, the only way you can remain steadfast on the Christian path and faithful to your call and your mission in love, is to take heed of Christ's instructions to us about himself, in John 15:1-4, 5, and 7-8, NIV,

> "I am the true vine, and my Father is the gardener. He cuts off every vine in me that bears no fruit, while every branch that does bear fruit he prunes so that it will be even more fruitful… Remain in me, and I will remain in you. No branch can bear fruit by itself; it must remain in the vine. Neither can you bear fruit unless you remain in me…; apart from me you can do nothing…If you remain in me and my words remain in you, ask whatever you wish, and it will be given you. This is to my Father's glory, that you bear much fruit, showing yourselves to be my disciples."

These are very important instructions, incentives, and favors, with power, for God's kingdom ministry through Christ Jesus, for all obedient, redeemed, and righteous human souls on fire for God.

Therefore, St. Paul, one of Jesus Christ's greatest disciples of the New Testament biblical church era said, (about his ministry-call and mission), in Philippians 3:13-14, in the NKJV Bible, "One thing I do, forgetting those things which are behind [the past], I press towards the goal for the prize of the upward call of God in Christ Jesus."

God has called and chosen all the redeemed and the righteous born-again believers in Christ Jesus, to humble themselves for a life of anointed service—when He called them out of darkness into His marvelous light, to empower them for His Kingdom ministry. He expects them to go out into the world to evangelize, (as His disciples did in biblical times), through the power of the Holy Spirit and of "Jesus Christ's Great Commission"* anointing in Mark 16:15-18.

Therefore, "Our Daily Bread" September 7th 1997 issue said about God's call and our mission, through Christ Jesus, "Serving Christ under [God's] law is a duty; serving Christ under love is a delight."

Now, if you are not specially called, chosen, and anointed by God, and covered under the blood of Jesus Christ and His "Great Commission" for service, as well as possessing the power and gifts or fruit of the Holy Spirit, you are surely wasting your time in ministry. For this is what God's Kingdom ministry is all about. So consequently, if your ministry motive is false, or without God's anointing especially, every redeemed or righteous born-again believer and Satan's disciples will really sense and observe whether you are truly called, chosen, anointed, and sent by God through Christ Jesus, to serve God alone, and you chose to serve a different master (Satan).

Matthew 6:24, in the NIV Bible, says, "No one can serve two masters. Either he will hate the one and love the other, or he will be devoted to the one and despise the other. You cannot serve both God and money [or God and Satan]."

So at this point, take note here what the Holy Bible says about our financial dealings when serving God. And this teaching explained here refer to both the redeemed and the righteous: It teaches that money is not the root of all evil, but "The love of money is the root or source of all kinds of evil" (1 Timothy 6:10, NIV). So 1 Timothy 6:10 continues, "Some people, eager for money [in ministry], have wandered from the faith and pierced themselves with many griefs," (just like Judas Iscariot, who betrayed Jesus for 30 pieces of silver).

And therefore, 1Timothy 3:1-2 and verse 8 says, about God's servants: "If anyone sets his heart on being an overseer, [a special leader in ministry], he desires a noble task... Now the overseer must be without reproach... and must not pursue dishonest gain."

Believe it or not, the love of money has had many believers to lose their souls to Satan. So in Timothy 3:3, St. Paul said this very candidly and strictly to Timothy, and cautioned him, because he was a young convert who was very zealous, and a redeemed believer in ministry for Christ Jesus.

Note well: When Jesus called Peter and Andrew for God's Kingdom ministry, they did not make money the main issue of their life; for they abandoned their fishing nets immediately—their main source of income and livelihood—and they followed Jesus instantly; for something radically and spiritually mysterious had happened to them. They became changed men in the twinkle of an eye: they no longer had the desire to serve the creature (Satan), as in the past, through the love of money, (Satan's bait), but only to serve the Creator (God), through Christ Jesus.

Subsequently, with the disciples' established frame of mind, Jesus chose the opportunity to command and empower them later on for further earthly Kingdom ministry. This happened just before He ascended to His heavenly Father.

Jesus said to them, "All authority in heaven and on earth has been given to me. Therefore go and make disciples of all nations, baptizing them... and teaching them to obey everything I have commanded you...." (Matthew 28:18-20, NIV).

Note well: With authority comes power, protection, and responsibility; and Jesus gave and still gives all the redeemed and the righteous born-again believers that same "power," "authority," "protection," and "responsibility," which God gave Him. And, as "a child of God"* who has been "Blood-washed,"* I know that Jesus has done the same for me and other believers too, for our mission on earth. For the same signs and wonders which happened in His days are still happening today: the redeemed and the righteous believers are still manifesting and performing the same miracles of healing, casting out of demons, raising the dead etc. etc., "in Jesus' mighty name."

Remember that Jesus said in John 14:12-14, in the NIV Bible, "I tell you the truth, anyone who has faith in me will do what I have been doing. He will do even greater things than these, because I am going to the Father. You may ask me for anything in my name, and I will do it."

So this is as much for our kingdom ministry with "power" for Christ Jesus, through "His Great Commission" (Matthew 28:18-20, and Mark 16:15-18).

Jesus has also called and commissioned all the redeemed and the righteous to be "the salt of the earth" and "the light of the world," in ministry: two other very important charges for us to fulfill our mission, for God's Kingdom on earth.

Jesus says to us in Matthew 5:13 in the NIV Bible, "You are the salt of the earth. But if salt loses its saltiness, how can it be made salty again? It is no longer good for anything, except to be thrown out and trampled by men."

As the salt of the earth we know that we should make everything we partake or participate in better, or leave it in a better condition—just as salt gives flavor and better taste to tasteless food. Therefore, all believers have been charged by God and Jesus with a mission to build, improve, and preserve, a better world—just like salt does to tasteless food. But if like salt we have become tasteless, it means that we have become useless and morally corrupt, (in human terms), or have become practicing sinners. And so, of what use are we now to humanity in God's Kingdom ministry?

When a redeemed or righteous believer becomes like tasteless salt, it is because he wallows deeply in sin, or other kinds of worldly corruption. But never mind, God still loves him; for God loves the sinner but He hates his sin. And again, God does not want or wish that any one of us should perish in hell, but come to repentance (2 Peter 3:9). God is still and always looking out for the "backsliders"* and the unredeemed to come to Him. And only repentance from our sin can restore or repair our sin-sick or corrupt body and souls. Furthermore, God is a God of grace and mercy, and of second chances. He can transform and reform the vilest sinner or backslider who is a mass of tasteless salt but truly believes in Jesus and repents, into a Christ-like person once more, who will become tasty and fit again for Kingdom ministry. May God be praised!

For many years I have heard some preachers say, that God is always married to the backsliders and will never divorce them. What do you think they mean by this affirmation? They simply mean that God's covenant with backsliders who were once practicing born-again believers, and had accepted Christ Jesus as their "Lord and personal savior," is like His covenant with his repeatedly unfaithful people (Israel), of biblical times; for God does not go back on His word. He is faithful! Or, plainly speaking, "He is not a man that he should lie; nor a son of man, that he should change his mind" (Numbers 23:19). He is a covenant keeping God!

I too, have been a backslider at one time in my ministry for Christ Jesus. And, most times, my continual contrite prayers and sincere humble repentance during daily devotions, have saved me from God's wrath; and His grace and mercy has helped me to remain steadfast on the path of righteousness and salvation, through my faith in Christ Jesus. The Holy Spirit and my daily meditation on God's Holy Word have also continually kept renewing my mind, body, soul, and spirit, by convicting, convincing, counselling, consoling, guiding, directing, teaching, and sanctifying me daily, so as to keep me ready for the Lord's return.

James 5:16, in the NIV Bible, says, "The prayer of a righteous man, [and a redeemed man I add], is powerful and effective."

The parable of "The Prodigal Son," (or "The Lost Son)" in Luke 15:11-31, and the scenario of King David's crime in 2 Samuel, highlights how God is so very loving and merciful to a repentant sinner and a backslider, who sincerely repents of his sin with a humble and contrite heart. Please read it yourself!

Psalm 107:1, in the NIV Bible, says, "Give thanks to the Lord, for he is good; his love endures forever."

And Psalm 103:8-14, in the NIV Bible, says,

> "The Lord is compassionate and graceous, slow to anger, abounding in love. He will not always accuse, nor will he harbor his anger forever; he will not treat us as our sins deserve, or repay us according to our iniquities. For as high as the heavens is above the earth, so great is his love for those who fear him; as far as the east is from the west, so far has he removed our transgressions from us. As a father has compassion on his children, so the Lord has compassion on those who fear him."

No matter how messed-up you and I are or have been by our sin, as with the Prodigal Son and King David, God never gives up on us. I have learnt this truth through practical experience, having been a backslider also, and a mass of tasteless salt at some time in my Christian walk with God. All that God desires of us when we have been first redeemed and subsequently back-slide, is to repent again and return to the path of righteousness quickly.

The Lord says, in Isaiah 43:18-19, "Forget the former things; do not dwell on the past. See, I am doing a new thing [in your life]! Now it springs up; do you not perceive it? I am making a way in the desert and streams in the wasteland [for you, I add]."

You just have to continue being "the salt of the earth" and "the light of the world!" And hold up the banner of righteousness for Christ Jesus.

Then, as "the light of the world," Jesus says that our mission after He has called us and chosen us is "to shine" (Matthew 5:16). And since we too have been called and chosen, our mission is to shine brightly so that the kingdom of unrighteousness (or Satan's domain of evil and darkness) will be eclipsed and dispelled, and "God's kingdom of Light and Truth" will prevail and overcome all unrighteousness.

Just as a candle when lighted and lifted up unhindered will give light for everyone to see, a disciple of Christ Jesus has to shine for all men to see his good deeds and praise God. His light should be like that of a lighthouse, or like a city on a hill-top which cannot be hidden, says Matthew 5:14-16, NIV.

In short, after all that has been previously said about the redeemed and righteous disciples' call and mission for God through Christ Jesus for Kingdom ministry, I wish to say here that I too have been called and commissioned in just the same way as some of the early prophets. I am referring especially to the prophets Jeremiah and Samuel.

Like Jeremiah and Samuel, I was called and chosen very early, for I was only 8 years old and responded immediately. But not every human soul on fire for God has been called and chosen at the same age, and out of the same situation and circumstances.

Since I was only a child, I did not know or realize that God had already chosen me for Kingdom ministry from my mother's womb. I only knew that I was called. For, as Holy Scripture says in Matthew 22:14, "Many are called, but few are chosen."

When God called the prophet Jeremiah, as in Jeremiah 1:5, He said to him, "Before I formed you in the womb I knew you, before you were born I set you apart; I appointed you as a prophet to the nations"—likewise myself.

So as time passed by (after God called me), His fire ignited in me by the power of the Holy Spirit and His Holy Word, grew so intense in me, like in Jeremiah, that I left every pleasure of the world behind—like St. Peter and Andrew in Matthew 4:20—to follow the straight and narrow way (God's way). I was then 18 years old and filled with enthusiasm and spiritual wonder.

Subsequently, at the age of 22 years, I took a break in my studies to do missionary work, because I experienced a spirit of doubt and anxiety (or fear) about my vocation to the priesthood. Consequently, I asked myself whether I was in the right place and pursuing the right goal: one of Satan's tricks which God turned around for my good in the long run. And it was then I began to understand and cherish more specially, the truths and power in and of Psalm 23:1-4, and Matthew 16:24, respectively.

Psalm 23:1-4, in the NIV Bible, says,

> "The Lord is my shepherd, I shall not want … [and note well what follows onwards that I put in single quote]: 'He restores my soul. He guides me in paths of righteousness for his name sake. Even though I walk through the valley of the shadow of death, I will fear no evil, for you are with me; your rod and your staff, they comfort me'."

And most important, what Jesus says in Matthew 16:24, NIV, "If anyone would come after me, he must deny himself, [leave family, worldly riches and pleasures, and other personal interests behind], and take up his cross and follow me: [surrender his life to Jesus]. For whoever wants to save his life [or pursue personal gain], will lose it; but whoever loses his life for me will find it"— receive all God's earthly and heavenly Kingdom riches.

So after denying myself for Jesus by denouncing worldly gain, I almost lost my health for God's sake—at least so I thought, and so it seemed to me then. But contrary to this belief, in God's spiritual timing, my health was completely restored: I was made whole and abundantly blessed. IF HE DID IT FOR ME, HE CAN DO IT FOR YOU TOO; FOR, "WITH GOD ALL THINGS ARE POSSIBLE" (Matthew 19:26, NIV); and, "EVERYTHING IS POSSIBLE FOR HIM WHO BELIEVES" (Mark 9:23, NIV).

I went through the valley of the shadow of death; but, as Psalm 23:4 says, Jesus ("The Good Shepherd") was always there with me, to guide, protect, and restore my soul, body, spirit, and mind, even when Satan seemed to be having his own way in some of my inexplicable and unjust situations. Truly, Jesus' peace and protection, through His rod and staff, and the Holy Spirit's counsel, guidance, power, and comfort, kept me safe, composed, and calm. And from then, until presently, I have lacked nothing and have always had God's protection as a redeemed and righteous human soul. King David, God's anointed and heartfelt friend, and a redeemed and righteous believer, says in Psalm 27:1-3, GNB,

> "The Lord is my light and my salvation, I will fear no one. The Lord protects me from all danger, I will never be afraid. When evil men attack me and try to kill me, they stumble and fall. Even if a whole army surrounds me, I will not be afraid; even if enemies attack me, I will still trust God"—for God will always protect me."

And he also says in Psalm 37:25, NIV, "I was young and now I am old, yet I have never seen the righteous forsaken or their children begging for bread."

So until now, I fear no evil; and I believe and trust in all God's promises and blessings in the Holy Bible, for the protection and provisions of the righteous and the redeemed, including God's powerful anointing for Kingdom ministry.

I have many other testimonies of God's and Jesus Christ's loving-kindness and protection in my lifetime, as a young Roman Catholic priest (or seminarian), as a minister and lay reader in the Anglican (or Episcopal) Church, and out in the world. All I can say now in retirement, after these experiences is: What Satan and his disciples meant for my defeat and destruction in my youth, God turned it around for my good fortune and favor in my latter days.

I therefore praise, bless, and thank the Blessed Trinity, for grace, mercy, peace, protection, joy, provision, and all other favors in my lifetime.

"Our Daily Bread" issue of October 22nd 1999 says, "There is no education like adversity."

Therefore, I categorically state here that all the fore-mentioned biblical assurances and blessings for the redeemed and the righteous which I will deal with later, can be summed up in Psalm 23:6 as: "Surely goodness and [God's] love will follow me [and all the redeemed and the righteous] all the days of my [our] life, and I [we] will dwell in the house of the Lord forever."

In my missionary work for God's Kingdom, I have had many dangerous experiences with Satan and his disciples. But Psalm 23:1-4, Psalm 91:10-11, Psalm 34:19, and Matthew 16:24, have kept me inspired, safe, consoled, comforted, and blessed by God. Now, I just wish to add one more Psalm to my fore-mentioned list, which is another important powerful Psalm (Psalm 27:1-3). I think it is just as awesome and powerful for the protection of the redeemed and righteous.

Psalm 27:1-3 and verse 5 says,

> "The Lord is my light and my salvation—whom shall I fear? The Lord is the stronghold of my life—of whom shall I be afraid? When evil men advance against me to devour my flesh, when my enemies and foes attack me, they will stumble and fall. Though an army besiege me, my heart will not fear; though war break out against me, even then will I be confident... For in the day of trouble he will keep me safe in his dwelling..."

Sadly, I temporarily neglected God and all the fore-mentioned Psalms and Scripture protection assurances, when I returned to the secular world at the age of 28 years. Obviously, it was because I had backslidden, or say, fallen from God's grace and favor by wallowing deeply in sin (or fornication), like a practicing-sinner.

Subsequently, the Holy Spirit and God's Holy Word intervened by convicting, arresting, and convincing me of my sin, in October 1981. I remember it as clearly as though it happened today. I was full of guilt and shame, and immediately repented of my sin. This also means that I had a personal encounter with Jesus Christ, and repented of my sin; following which I accepted, confessed, and professed Him, as my Lord and personal savior.

Since then, I have remained "saved and sanctified" by the grace and mercy of God, as "a redeemed sinner," or "a blood-washed sinner," or a "saint," as St. Paul puts it. And all these preceding terms are applicable to and for "a repentant sinner," who has been saved by God's grace. St. Paul called all the repentant sinners who have been "blood-washed" or saved by Jesus, "saints" (Ephesians 1:15, 18; 6:18; Philemon 1:7; and 1 Corinthians 6:2).

Peter and Andrew, when called by Jesus in Matthew 4:18-20, also had a born-again experience like me; for they were instantly transformed from within when called, and immediately followed Jesus. This personal encounter made them "saints."

I left the world for the last time at 31 years old, and returned to the foot of the cross (my first love). Once again, I became "a redeemed human soul on fire for God."

Some years later, I was ordained a licensed lay reader and minister in the Anglican Church, and journeyed there for 23 years, before the Lord called me again to a different ministry. This different ministry entailed the voluntary teaching of "Character Building through Christian Education, for Youth," in some southern schools on the island of St. Lucia, W.I. And when this program ended, I was then a retiree from my regular secular Job as a business clerk / supervisor. I now do witnessing for Jesus as a Sunday school teacher of adults, at "Born Again Revival Tabernacle Church," and also engage in world outreach evangelism through inspirational writing.

This ministry is so very important to me, that I quote from "Our Daily Bread" issue of July 15th 1988: "If you [or me] keep rejecting the 'come' of salvation, you [or me] will have to accept the 'depart' of damnation."

And, as C. S. Lewis said, "To walk out of God's will is to walk into nowhere."

Let me testify here to you that since I obeyed God's will and last call for ministry, I have experienced many better and brighter days and years than in my youth. For the peace of Christ and the Holy Spirit's comfort and counsel consoles me always, and keeps me youthful and strong like an eagle, and like a tree planted by the river water. And because Almighty God gave me a wise, loving, God-fearing, and encouraging wife (or helpmate), I am able to easily maintain, sustain, and enjoy, my final call and ministry for God's Kingdom, as a redeemed human soul on fire.

Once a redeemed, baptized, born-again believer has taken up ministry for God, through Christ Jesus, there should be no turning back—even though the road gets very rough. Ministry should only end when Almighty God calls us home (through death). For God's call for ministry is a very serious business, and a dedicated, ceaseless battle against Satan and his cohorts, until our life ends.

Luke 9:62, in the NIV Bible, says, "No one who puts his hand to the plow and looks back is fit for service in the kingdom of God."

I have already asked Almighty God for forgiveness for withdrawing my hands (or backsliding) from "the plow,"* after being called and chosen for Kingdom ministry in my youth. These were the years when I became like tasteless and useless salt, which was fit for nothing but only to be thrown away and trampled on (Matthew 5:13).

God pardoned me, saved me, and restored my sin-sick body, mind, soul, and spirit, and made me whole again—through the precious blood of Jesus Christ which was shed for my sins and others on Calvary's wooden cross. His unconditional love, grace, and mercy, has set me free. Surely, He is a God of mercy and compassion, and a God of second and many chances.

I now pray that the Holy Spirit's power, fruit, counsel, comfort, guidance, and inspiration, along with the power of God's Holy Word and Jesus Christ's biblical teachings, about salvation and eternal life, peace, love, joy, forgiveness, compassion, true freedom, and deliverance, will continue to rest, remain, abide, sustain, guide, maintain, and protect my family and I, in these latter years of my retirement, as I continue to spread Jesus Christ's gospel message among all humanity. For as Romans 1:16 says in the NIV, "I am not ashamed of the gospel [of Jesus Christ], because it is the power of God for the Salvation of everyone who believes...."

And Jesus also says in Mark 8:38 of the NIV Bible, "If anyone is ashamed of me and my words in this adulterous and sinful generation, the Son of Man will be ashamed of him when he comes in his Father's glory with the holy angels."

No one can love God without serving Him. And, as "Our Daily Bread" July 18th 1988 issue puts it: "If loving God means serving Him, he who abandons himself to God [in love and service, I add], will never be abandoned by God."

For, God is faithful to His promises, and His word is final. All that He asks of us is our OBEDIENCE, FAITHFULNESS, HUMILITY, WORSHIP, PRAISE AND THANKSGIVING; so give Him all the honor, praise and glory, with thanksgiving, that He rightly deserves. These are the greatest lessons that I have learnt about "GOD'S CALL AND OUR MISSION." And, as I acknowledged these truths, I was able to worship Him "in spirit and in truth;" for there is no other God like Him. He is the ONLY ONE, TRUE, EVERLASTING, OMNIPOTENT, OMNISCIENT, OMNIPRESENT, JUST, LOVING, MERCIFUL, and AWESOME LIVING GOD. "All the other gods are the works of men," says one song writer.

Jesus Christ's gospel message is "God's power unto salvation," for all those who believe and diligently seek Him. And it is that same gospel message power which helps all the righteous and redeemed who are anointed to rescue fallen humanity.

So, as Jesus Christ said to the unbelieving religious leaders and people about Himself in biblical times—but especially to Phillip, in John 14:10, NIV: "Believest thou not that I am in the Father, and the Father in me? ... The Father that dwelleth in me, he doeth the works"—works of righteousness. This is the question and answer that the redeemed and the righteous should entertain with many unbelievers who doubt their calling and anointing capability, especially in their own home town. For, this is the same reason and more, that Jesus Christ did not perform any miracles in His own home-town: the people there were very critical, slanderous, and unbelieving about Him, as God's Anointed One--likewise for you and me.

"May God have mercy on them!"

3

WHO ARE WE THROUGH CHRIST JESUS

Even though we are highly esteemed by others in this world, God sees us only as dust and ashes, before we accept Jesus Christ as our Lord and Personal Savior—because that is where and what we were made from, and what we will return to finally (Gen. 3:19). Had it not been for God's love and mercy by sending His beloved Son (Jesus Christ) to suffer and die for us and in our place on Calvary's wooden cross, we would all perish in hell for our sins. But, when we became born-again believers through the power of Christ Jesus and the Holy Spirit, we became joint heirs with Christ, citizens of heaven, and sons and daughters of God. So that believers are Jesus Christ's "church militants"* on earth, who have been redeemed (or saved and sanctified) by His precious blood shed for us on Calvary's wooden cross. And we therefore have a special mission to perform for Christ Jesus on earth: we are supposed to "evangelize"* for Him whilst being "the Salt of the earth" and "the Light of the world," and, at the same time, we must work out our own salvation with fear and trembling. I repeat, "and work out our own salvation with fear and trembling," as St. Paul says in Philippians 2:12. For, even though God's mercy, grace, and loving-kindness towards us never fails, He maintains His power, justice, holiness, righteousness, and His awesomeness.

Now since "sin" is the most controversial issue of the Christian life, as regards "the salvation of all humanity," I will deal with it first, so that we can view ourselves in the proper perspective—particularly, who we are today through Christ Jesus, after God found us in a mess and transformed us, or made us whole again: through His Justification, sanctification, the peace of Christ Jesus, and His special grace and mercy.

Sin is a deadly disease, which is sometimes viewed as and called, a cancer or leprosy of the human soul. It physically and spiritually disorients us, and finally separates and destroys every careless, shameless, and disobedient believer and unbeliever from God—needless to mention about how it specially disables the awesome powers of every redeemed and righteous human soul on fire for God. So every redeemed and righteous born-again believer has to be very mindful and careful about this.

Many deadly diseases are the results of our own sin, or sins, because of an unhealthy lifestyle (like sexual perversion), which we perpetrate, or "a generational curse"* which we inherit from our family lineage, or God's allowed Satanic affliction on us like on Job, (in the book of Job, in the Holy Bible), to test our faith, or, like in St. Paul's case in 2 Corinthians 12:9, to keep us humble.

God said to St. Paul, in 2 Corinthians 12:9, that He will not heal him of his disease—the thorn in his flesh—because His (God's) grace is sufficient for him; and that God's power is made perfect in Paul's weakness. When I studied this, I felt it difficult to believe that maybe I would have to settle for a situation or answer like this also, despite the fact that I know that God's answers to our prayers are "YES," "NO," or "WAIT." I decided not to accept St. Paul's "NO" for my answer, but rather, "YES," or "WAIT"—based on Psalm 34, verse 19, in the KJV Bible, where King David (God's anointed and close friend) said, "Many are the afflictions of the righteous; but the Lord delivereth him out of them all"—NOT SOME, BUT ALL! And I found consolation.

And in the GNB version, Psalm 34:20, King David continues: "The Lord preserves him completely, [both the righteous and the redeemed]."

King David also said in Psalm 103:2-3, in the GNB version, "Praise the Lord, my soul, and do not forget how kind he is. He forgives all my sins and heals all my diseases."

God does not wish that any of us should remain and perish in sin or of our diseases; for even though He is a God of justice, He is also eternally merciful, compassionate, and loving. He is a God of grace and mercy also, and His mercy endures forever, says Psalm 103:8. When He punishes or humbles us through sickness and trials, it is to draw us closer to Him in humility, (like He did to St. Paul), and to secure our salvation and eternal life; so that through our repentance, His forgiveness, His justification, and sanctification of us, with our worship, praise, and thanksgiving for Him, we will experience His goodness. And so, He does not keep on rebuking us forever, says Psalm 103:9-10. He seasonally heals us, lightens our burdens, takes them away, or gives us only what we can bear, for He is a God of second and many chances. But do not try his patience; He is also a God who punishes to bring us back to our right senses. I dare say to you also, look at how many times He punished and forgave, and still blessed His chosen people (Israel of Biblical times), repeatedly, even though they were continually very disloyal and disobedient to Him, by worshiping pagan Gods. You and I are no different to them, for many of us still have idols (or things and people) that we put before Him in our lives. I am sure that we are unable to count how many times that we have worshipped idols that have caused us to rebel or sin against Him and He has not consumed but only punished us. On one occasion, God even repented of his decision and action, (humanly speaking), when He punished and destroyed the very sinful generation of wicked people in the days of Noah, and He smelled the pleasant aroma of Noah's sacrificial offering afterwards. God does not want any of us to perish.

So God said in Genesis 8:21, in the NIV, "Never again will I curse the ground because of man, even though every inclination of his heart is evil from childhood. And never again will I destroy all living creatures [by water] as I have done."

Therefore, after reading the fore-mentioned Psalms and Scripture passages for many years, with prayers of praise, supplication, thanksgiving, and meditation, I waited patiently with faith in God, and became so positively resolute with hope, that I finally affirmed my complete healing, and God healed my disease and forgave all my sins (Psalm 103:2-3). So I firmly believe that He can and will also do the same for me again in the future, as well as for you too, if you have faith.

Consequently, I drew strength from my past afflictions, to face my recently healed cancer affliction, by recalling Ecclesiastes 3:1 in the NKJV Bible, which says, "To everything there is a season, and a time to every purpose under the heaven."

My season eventually and finally came, through the "divine intervention"* of God's help through Christ Jesus—from the many godly persons and Christians who sincerely lived under "the New Dispensation"* of God's law of grace and mercy, and faith in Jesus Christ. God used the expertise of many faith-filled doctors and other medical staff, and heard the prayers of my church intercessors, family and friends, and the relentless prayers of my faithful, faith-filled, Holy-Spirit-filled and loving wife, who stood at my side and in heaven's gap for me. And I am completely healed now. I therefore give God through the power of Christ Jesus, all the honor, thanks, praise, and glory, for all the talents and prayers of His faith-filled people, including mine. I can now affirm that I am indeed a cancer survivor. May God richly bless all of them according to their needs and His riches in glory!

St. Paul says in Philippians 4:6-7, in the NIV Bible, "Do not be anxious about anything, but in everything, by prayer and petition, with thanksgiving, present your request to God. And the peace of God, which transcends all understanding, will guard your hearts and your minds [and body, I add] in Christ Jesus."

Now even though we are no longer under the powers of "the Old Dispensation," or "the Mosaic Law," (the Ten Command-ments), which brought death, sickness, and condemnation to hell-fire for all condemned sinners, we must still observe its power to destroy us if we continue to be practicing sinners. Only when we live under God's law of grace and mercy through faith in Christ Jesus we are safe and free.

This is how St. Paul puts it in Romans 5:20-21, in the NIV Bible: "The [Mosaic] law was added so that the trespass might increase. But where sin increased, grace increased all the more, so that, just as sin reigned in death, so also grace might reign through righteousness to bring eternal life [or a special spiritual blessing] through Jesus Christ Our Lord."

So we know now that even when sin increases and grace in-crease, we should not persevere or continue in unrighteousness. For Romans 6:23 in the NIV Bible says, "For the wages of sin is death, but the gift of God is eternal life in Christ Jesus Our Lord."

It was God, through Christ Jesus, who straightened out my life by saving me, and setting me free from, disease, and the fear of death, to have a life of peace, faith, righteousness, health, joy, self-control, humility, love, compassion, forgiveness and grace: He gave me back "abundant life". I only had to repent of my sin and cast all my burdens on Jesus; and, as I cast my cares on Jesus, He took care of everything (Matthew 11:28-30). IF HE DID IT FOR ME, HE CAN DO IT FOR YOU TOO; FOR JESUS IS THE GREATEST PHYSI-CIAN, AND THE PHYSICIAN OF ALL PHYSICIANS!

Romans 5:19, in the NIV Bible, says, "Just as through the dis-obedience of one man [Adam] the many were made sinners, so also through the obedience of one man [Jesus Christ] the many were made righteous."

But our righteousness earned through redemption (or deliverance from sin through Christ Jesus) will profit us nothing, if we persist or continue again as a "practicing sinner,"* (as I said before), after being "saved."* We must break the old habit of regular sinning, through the power of regular prayer and meditation, and occasional fasting, with daily repentance and asking God for forgiveness as soon as the opportunity arises. This is how I live my life in righteousness daily, to avoid becoming a sin-sick soul and body; for in this experience, soul, mind, and spirit affect body, and vice versa, a sin-sick body affects soul, mind, and spirit. And this is also how I always try to preserve my salvation daily, because I do not know the hour or minute when God will call on me (through death), or Christ will come again to judge all the living and the dead.

Sin carries with it more deadly consequences and afflictions than even the most deadly human diseases, such as cancer, aids, covid-19, depression, leprosy, etc. And only God, through Christ Jesus, can affect a complete cure with no side effects for all of them.

Sometimes, even when or whilst waiting for a death sentence or decree from a physician for a deadly disease such as aids, or cancer, sin's deadlier decrees and results from them, like depression, despair, fear, or worry and anxiety, can cause some persons to commit pre-meditated suicide—even though the primary or most important desire of every human being is for his own self-preservation and survival.

Thank God for early detection, healing, and deliverance, from the generational curse of cancer—through the power of Christ Jesus, the prayers and help of the saints and righteous persons, and the many dedicated, righteous, and humble medical personnel. Otherwise, I could have been a victim of its deadly circumstances. If we always and only trust and have faith in God through Christ Jesus, we will always be overcomers. When prayer and faith in God through Christ Jesus mixes with the expertise of many humble or righteous physicians, and the intercessory prayers of the saints along with the help of many righteous persons (or good Samaritans), miracles can and will always happen. I recognized the mind, heart, and hand of Jesus in all of them who assisted me. Jesus was not too late to save me; He appeared right on time and in time, for a repentant sinner like me. And He can do the same for you too. All you have to do, apart from your early regular check-ups, is repent of your sin or sins, and trust God through Christ Jesus for a miraculous healing (or deliverance), in faith; for sometimes, sin (or a generational curse) can be the impediment or cause of our disease. So sin must also be dealt with first, sometimes, and healing will come next and easily. Jesus demonstrated this phenomenon in Luke 5:17-26, when He said to the paralyzed man, "Your sins are forgiven," before proceeding to affect his healing.

We must also always humble ourselves and pray for deliverance when we have a problem or need; for both God and Jesus detest proud persons. We must also admit that we have a problem and need a healing or deliverance, and go to Jesus just as we are (with all our burdens and sin, and with one plea), like the Publican (or tax collector) who went to the temple to pray (Luke 18:13, NIV). Then God will hear and answer our sincere prayer.

Because the tax collector felt so penitent, unworthy, and humble, he stood at the entrance of the temple and did not go inside like everyone else; he just stood at the entrance and said this simple and humble prayer to God: "God, have mercy on me, a sinner" (Luke 18:13, NIV).

We are all sinners; so just tell Jesus that you need His forgiveness. Tell Him also that you need His help to carry your burden or burdens. He will gladly and willingly help you, and you will find mercy, grace, healing, peace and rest for your soul and body (Matthew 11:28-30).

Proverbs 28:13, in the NIV Bible, says, "He who conceals his sins does not prosper, but whoever confesses and renounces them finds mercy." Then Satan's ploys and schemes will not trap you. Once more, I thank Almighty God in the name of Jesus, for His healing grace and mercy, and the "abundant life" that has been restored to me. Satan's ploys are no match for the Savior's power and plans for us.

Some people and friends said that I am a very lucky person—because both of my parents died of cancer—but I rather say that I am and will always be blessed by God; for God had already singled me out from my mother's womb for Kingdom ministry, and still singles me out today for special service–just as He did to the prophet Jeremiah.

In Jerimiah 5:1, in the NIV, God said to Jerimiah, "Before I formed you in the womb I knew you, before you were born I set you apart; I appointed you as a prophet to the nations."

Therefore, I consider myself just as blessed as Jeremiah, and the leper in Luke 17: 11-19, who was healed by Jesus and he returned to give God thanks and praise through Christ Jesus. So I saw nothing better then and now, but to continue going to the house of God and give Him thanks and praise continually, and serve and worship Him in the beauty of holiness in His sanctuary. King David (the psalmist of Holy Scripture), has this to say about my experience, in Psalm 29:2, in the NIV Bible: "Ascribe to the Lord the glory due his name; worship the Lord in the splendor of his holiness."

And remember also what Jesus said to the healed leper who returned to give Him thanks and praise, in Luke 17:17-19: "Were not all [ten] cleansed? Where are the other nine? Was no one found to return and give praise to God except the foreigner? … Rise and go; your faith has made you whole."

Many people who have been forgiven of their sins (or sin) and were healed by God, through Christ Jesus, have never returned to give God thanks, praise, and worship. That is why the parable of the ten lepers is recorded in Luke 17:17-19, in the Holy Bible. It reminds us most times of our ingratitude for God's saving grace and mercy, His unconditional favor of healing, His loving-kindness, provision, and protection, the awesome power of Jesus Christ's powerful ministry in and through God's Church on earth, and the Holy Spirit-filled and Christ-commissioned ministry of the redeemed and righteous human souls on fire for God, depicted in Matthew 28:18-19, and Luke 16:15-16. Such negligence can also be considered an act of fear, doubt, and/or complacency, because some people are just too proud to testify about the power of God through Christ Jesus in their life—publicly and/or privately. They just don't want anyone to know that they had a deadly disease like cancer, mental illness, aids, leprosy, drug addiction, or alcoholism, etc., or a deplorable and shameful life-situation like Mary Magdalene (the prostitute), or like St. Paul (the serial killer), and the Lord healed or delivered them. And so, God does not get all the praise, honor, and glory that He so rightly deserves.

Jesus Christ says in Matthew 10:32-33, in the NIV Bible, "Whoever acknowledges me before man, I will acknowledge him before my Father in heaven. But whoever disowns me before man, I will disown him before my Father in heaven."

Holy Scriptures say that we can overcome these Satanic, pride-related, defeating emotions of worry, fear, tension, low self-esteem, doubt, shame, discouragement, and depression to not acknowledge God's healing and deliverance power in our lives, by proclaiming, witnessing, and confessing privately and publicly to others, "the power" of "the name" and "the blood of Jesus" to save, cleanse (or wash), protect, heal, and deliver us from sin, sickness, and all of our other burdens. And we must testify about and proclaim God's awesomeness and His goodness at all times. For

Satan tries to make us believe that we are hopeless and helpless with our burdens, trials, temptations and other problems, and that God's promises for "abundant life" in John 10:10, through Christ Jesus, is a lie—just to steal our joy. Consequently, he frequently uses backsliders, unbelievers, and even some practicing believers, to deceive, discourage, and trap us with fearful, deceitful, and doubtful mind-games, by reminding us of the difficult Christian life trials, sufferings, deaths, persecutions, worldly ridicule, and martyrdom that our predecessors have faced, as well as our past weaknesses, failures, and shameful deeds, which we have already repented of. But never mind when Satan does this. All that we need to do immediately is to rebuke him, by reminding him and his cohorts about God's punishment for them on Judgment Day (Revelation 20:1-3, and 7-15), and the destiny of the redeemed and righteous.

It was St. John, (Jesus Christ's exiled apostle on the Greek island of Patmos in the Mediterranean sea), who spoke about God's punishment for Satan, and the destiny and powers of the redeemed and righteous martyred human souls on fire for God on Judgement Day. St. John remarked,

> "And I saw an angel coming down out of heaven, having the key to the Abyss [hell] and holding in his hand a great chain. He seized the dragon, that ancient serpent who is the devil, or Satan, and bound him for a thousand years. He [God's angel] threw him into the Abyss, and locked and sealed it over him, to keep him from deceiving the nations anymore until the thousand years were ended. After that, he must be set free for a short time.
>
> [And St. John continued], I saw thrones on which were seated those who had been given authority to judge, [including the redeemed and the righteous souls (or saints) who were on fire for God on earth]. And I saw the

souls of those who had been beheaded, [the martyrs], because of their testimony for Jesus and because of the word of God. They had not worshiped the beast or his image [Satan's representatives and symbols on earth], and had not received his mark on their foreheads or their hands. They came to life and reigned with Christ a thousand years.

[Then] When the thousand years are over, Satan will be released from his prison and will go out to deceive the nations in the four corners of the earth to gather them for battle [against God's people]. In number they are like the sand on the seashore. They marched across the breadth of the earth and surrounded the camp of God's people, the city he loves. But fire came down from heaven and devoured them. And the devil who deceived them was thrown into the lake of burning sulfur, where the beast and the false prophet had been thrown. They will be tormented day and night for ever and ever" (Revelation 20:1-4 and 7-15, NIV).

Now knowing all that about Satan when he attacks you [a believer], you must also quickly remember to affirm with great certainty and solid conviction about yourself that,

(a) "No weapon forged against [you] will prevail, and [you] will refute every tongue that accuses [you]. This is the heritage of the servants of the Lord, and this is their vindication from me, declares the Lord" (Isaiah 54:17, NIV).

Because,

(b) "If anyone is in Christ he is a new creation; the old

[self] has gone, the new has come! All this is from God who reconciled us to himself through Christ Jesus and gave us the ministry of reconciliation..." (Corinthians 5:17-18, NIV). And say,

(c) "I have been crucified with Christ and I no longer live, but Christ lives in me. The life I live in the body, I live by faith in the Son of God, who loved me and gave himself for me" (Galatians 2:20, NIV). So,

(d) "By the grace of God I am what I am" (1 Corinthians 11:10, NIV). And,

(e) "Therefore, there is now no condemnation for those who are in Christ Jesus, because through Christ Jesus the law of the Spirit of life set [you and me] free from the law of sin and death" (Romans 8:1-2, NIV).

So take note, all redeemed and righteous believers. Don't let Satan and his deceptive disciples discourage you or quench your Holy Spirit fire and your zeal for God's Kingdom ministry through Christ Jesus; for "The joy of the Lord is your strength" (Nehemiah 8:10, NIV). And "IN ALL THINGS, WE ARE MORE THAN CONQUORERS THROUGH HIM (CHRIST) WHO LOVES US" (Romans 8:37, NIV). When God healed and cleansed me (a sinful leper), at the age of 31 years old, I was so full of joy that I could not contain my emotions—all because His Holy Word became rooted in my heart even deeper than before. So, like the prophet Jeremiah, in the book of Jeremiah, Chapter 20, and verse 9 of the NIV Bible, I could then and now still say, "His word is in my heart like a fire, a fire shut up in my bones. I am weary of holding it in; indeed I cannot."

Since then, prayer, meditation, fasting, teaching, preaching, and evangelistic inspirational writing have been a normal and regular way of life for me. And I have come to realize that my inspirational writing with its world evangelistic outreach approach, is also very fulfilling and answering one of the most important parts of Jesus Christ's command to all His redeemed and righteous disciples, when He said in Mark 16:15-16, and Matthew 28:19, respectively:

> "Go into the world and preach the good news to all creation. Whoever believes and is baptized will be saved, but whoever does not believe will be condemned" (Mark 16:15-16, NIV). And] "Therefore, go and make disciples of all nations ... teaching them to obey everything I have commanded you" (Matthew 28:19, NIV).

Right now, as I write to encourage and edify all the redeemed and righteous human souls on fire for God, my first book can be ordered from my home address in St. Lucia, W.I., and the other inspirational books can be ordered on-line from Barns and Noble, Amazon, Page Turner Press and Media, and Xlibris book stores, throughout the USA, Canada, Africa, and Europe—as well as in other countries where these book stores are established around the world. And my books are all specifically written for the purpose of evangelism.

Now let me get back on track about who we are through Christ Jesus!

The price that Jesus Christ paid for us by shedding His precious blood on Calvary's wooden cross was a sufficient ransom for our salvation and healing.

Jesus died for us, and in our place, so that we could have salvation and eternal life. This means that He died to set the whole world of us sinners free from the penalty for our sins. And how did He do this? He took all the blame, shame, sickness, and punishment for our sins upon Him, and imputed to us (or gave us) His righteousness in return. As a result of this one righteous act of His, God considers and declares (or proclaims) every humble and sincere repentant sinner "not guilty" of their sins, or sin. This act of exoneration by God is called "Justification."*

St. Paul therefore says in Romans 8:31-39, in the NIV Bible, "What, then, shall we say in response to this? If God is for us, who can be against us? He who did not spare his own Son but gave him up for us all—how will he not also, along with him, graciously give us all things? Who will bring a charge against those whom God has chosen? It is God who justifies. Who is he that condemns? Christ Jesus who died—more than that, who was raised to life— is at the right hand of God and is also interceding for us [always]. Who shall separate us from the love of Christ? ... No, in all things we are more than conquerors through him who loved us ... [Nothing] in all creation, will be able to separate us from the love of God that is in us through Christ Jesus our Lord."

Therefore, we must always remember that when we fall short of the mark of righteousness again, after our first repentance, Romans 8:34 says, Jesus Christ who died and was raised to life for us is at the right hand of God always interceding for us; so, nothing can separate us from the love of God through Christ Jesus. That is why I say gratefully, that Salvation is the first free gift and miracle of God to us and every redeemed born-again and righteous believer, through His grace and mercy.

Now what did being saved through Christ Jesus entail for me? It was basically repeating with a humble and contrite heart, and faith in Jesus Christ, "the sinner's prayer."*

I had to admit and confess to God with my mouth that I am a sinner, and ask Him to forgive me of my sin. Then, I had to believe in my heart and confess with my mouth that Jesus Christ is Lord; that He died to save me from my sin and condemnation to hell fire, and that God raised Him up from death after three days in the tomb. Then, Jesus did the remainder of the saving work along with God, after I repeated "the sinner's prayer"* for my salvation miracle. And, just like that, right there and then, through my faith in Jesus Christ, I felt as though a load was lifted from my shoulder, and an inexplicable peace came over me. Therefore, I knew that I was "saved."*

Holy Scripture says that our salvation or being saved has nothing to do with our own righteousness, goodness, integrity, or our good works alone; for Isaiah 64:6 says, "Our righteous acts are as filthy rags." Therefore, there is no way we can work for or earn our salvation by our own merits.

Salvation is a free gift from God, for all those who believe and willingly accept, claim, profess, and trust, Jesus Christ and His righteousness, in faith. We do not deserve it by our own merits; it is God's unconditional love and unmerited favor for us, through the power of Jesus Christ's shed blood and His death on Calvary's wooden cross.

I beseech you therefore, if you ever hear the beckoning voice of Jesus today, harden not your heart; tomorrow may be too late to accept such a precious gift as salvation. Let Jesus come and "sup with you" and accept Him into your heart "as your Lord and Personal Savior"—just as all believers did. He is always willing and able to give you His peace, love, joy, health, and every other good gift that He has promised in John 10:10, as God's package of and for "abundant life."

With all these precious gifts in you, including the seven-fold gifts or fruit of the Holy Spirit, and the resolute youthfulness of all those who wait on the Lord (God) through Christ Jesus, your strength will be renewed like the eagle's, and you shall run and not be weary, walk and never faint (Isaiah 40:29-31). And you will not be able to contain the fire and zeal within you that the prophet Jeremiah and I felt in our heart and bones, to do God's Kingdom ministry. Even in your old age you shall still be enthusiastic and bear fruit. Psalm 92:12-15, in the NIV Bible, says,

"The righteous will flourish like a palm tree, they will grow like the cedar of Lebanon; planted in the house of the Lord, they will flourish in the courts of our God. They will still bear fruit in old age, they will stay fresh and green, [a sign of youthfulness and strength], proclaiming, 'The Lord is upright; he is my Rock, and there is no wickedness in him.'"

Note well: When a redeemed and righteous human soul is on fire for God during Kingdom ministry, Jesus, the Holy Spirit, God, His angels, and all the forces of nature always unite and rally around him to protect him in the midst of life's storms and persecutions. This is a very powerful influence and consolation. If you don't believe me, just consider what Holy Scripture says will happen when just God and His holy angels alone operate to guide and protect the righteous and redeemed, in Psalm 91:9-16.

Psalm 91:9-16, in the NIV Bible, says,

"If you make the Most High your dwelling... then no harm will befall you, no disaster will come near your tent. For he [God] will give his angels concerning you to guard you in all your ways; they will lift you up in their hands, so that you will not strike your foot against a stone. You will tread upon the lion and the cobra; you will trample the great lion and the serpent."

And God continues, "Because he loves me... I will rescue him; I will protect him, for he acknowledges my name... I will be with him in trouble, I will deliver him and honor him... and show him my salvation."

And Psalm 91 also says that God protects the righteous and the redeemed from the deadly pestilence that stalks in darkness, and the plagues that destroy people at midday. He protects His beloved and chosen ones both day and night, against Satan and his disciples, just as He did to Jesus.

That is why God's anointed and righteous servant (King David) said in Psalm 23:4, NIV, "Even though I walk through the valley of the shadow of death, I will fear no evil, for you are with me; your rod and your staff, they comfort me."

Again, Holy Scripture says, that as we (the anointed redeemed and the righteous) store God's Holy Word in our heart and mind for battle against Satan, during our Kingdom ministry, or in ministry for Christ Jesus, it will not only be a lamp unto our feet and light unto our path, (Psalm 119:105), but can also be used as a two-edged sword (or a powerful weapon) to fight against Satan and his disciples. For a two-edged sword cuts both ways. And a Holy Scripture says, it cuts even right down to where bone and marrow meet. It cuts or inflicts a wound that both believers and unbelievers feel; and at this same time, it can heal, console, enlighten, deliver, encourage, restore peace, direct (as a compass does), protect, feed, and strengthen both the believer and unbeliever, and affect an unbeliever's redemption, as well as uproot and destroy the very foundations of Satan's Kingdom. By "foundations" I mean the areas within our lives where Satan has his "strongholds"* of sin, and his influence on us through the power of deception and temptation by worldly riches, power, sexual promiscuity, illegal drugs, alcohol abuse, witchcraft, magic, divination, etc., and the distortion of "the Gospel Truth," through false preachers and Satanic or false religious doctrine.

The Old Testament Holy Scriptures and Jesus Christ's Gospel truth-messages are the redeemed and the righteous' most powerful weapon against Satan and his disciples, apart from their faith in Almighty God. Jesus Christ demonstrated that in Matthew, Chapter 4, whilst He was being tempted in the desert by Satan, after fasting for forty days and forty nights. So studying or feeding on God's Word, and meditating, digesting, retaining, practicing, recalling, and timely applying it in all life situations against Satan, just as Jesus did, is the key to a believer's spiritual health, success, strength, power, true identity, and survival.

The Pharisees, Sadducees, Essenes, and other religious leaders of biblical times, in Jesus' days, as well as some of today's Pharisees, (or religious conservatives), found and still find it difficult to accept or tolerate the plain and naked truths explained in God's Holy Word. So even today, many powerful redeemed and righteous human souls on fire for God are still imprisoned and/or martyred, opposed, accused, rejected, and/or punished as scapegoats, for witnessing and ministering Jesus Christ's gospel truth message. Therefore, as a Christian or a redeemed and righteous human soul on fire for God, through Christ Jesus, you should expect nothing better from this world. Your fate has already been sealed like Jesus', especially in countries where there is no religious tolerance or freedom.

St. Peter puts it quite vividly in 1 Peter 2:19-21, in the NIV version,

> "For it is commendable if a man bears under the pain of unjust suffering because he is conscious of God. But how is it to your credit if you receive a beating for doing wrong and endure it? But if you suffer for doing good and you endure it [like Jesus, St. Paul, or St. Stephen], this is commendable before God. To this you were called, because Christ suffered for you, leaving you an example that you should follow in his footsteps."

Remember that the awesome ministry of the redeemed and the righteous human soul on fire for God, through Christ Jesus, is very rough sometimes—because Satan and his disciples are formidable challenges and forces for us to contend with. But do not be afraid; the power of the Blessed Trinity, [the Father (God), the Son (Jesus Christ), and the Holy Spirit], will always guide, protect, and comfort every born-again believer. For "God did not give us a spirit of timidity [or fear], but a spirit of power, of love and self-discipline, [or a sound mind, as the KJV puts it]."

God also said In Joshua 1:5 in the NIV, "I will never leave you nor forsake you."

And then after Jesus' death and resurrection, when He appeared to His hidden, huddled-together, frightened and discouraged disciples in an upper-room in Jerusalem, He said to them—just to encourage them to go out into the world again, to do Kingdom ministry without fear: "Peace I leave with you; my peace I give you. I do not give to you as the world gives. Do not let your heart be troubled and do not be afraid" (John 14:27, NIV).

He also said to His disciples concerning Kingdom ministry,

"I am the true vine, and my Father is the gardener. He cuts off every branch in me that bears no fruit, while every branch that does bear fruit he prunes so that it will be even more fruitful. You are already clean because of the word I have already spoken to you. Remain in me, and I will remain in you. No branch can bear fruit by itself; it must remain in the vine... If a man remains in me and I in him, he will bear much fruit; apart from me you can do nothing... If you remain in me and my words remain in you, ask whatever you wish and it will be given you. This is to my Father's glory, that you bear much fruit, showing yourself to be my disciples..." (John 15:1-8, NIV).

And He continued,

"If the world hates you, keep in mind that it hated me first. If you belonged to the world, it would love you as its own. As it is, you do not belong to the world, but I have chosen you out of the world. That is why the world hates you. Remember the words I spoke to you: No servant is greater than his master. If they persecuted me, they will persecute you also. If they obey my teaching, they will obey yours also. They will treat you this way because of my name, for they do not know the One who sent me... They hate me without reason... (John 15:18-21, NIV).

All this I have told you so that you will not go astray. They will put you out of the Synagogue [or church]; in fact a time is coming when anyone who kills you will think he is offering a sacrifice to God [just like some of the intolerant, radical, and fanatic religions and worldly governments did in biblical times, and are still doing in some countries today]. They will do such things because they have not known the Father or me. I have told you this, so that when the time comes you will remember that I warned you" (John 16:1-4, NIV).

And Jesus concludes His warning discourse to His disciples with these encouraging words of John 16:33: "I have told you these things, so that in me you may have peace. In this world you will have trouble. But take heart! I have overcome the world."

Therefore, we too can overcome the world; for "We can do all things through Christ who strengthens us" (Philippians 4:13); and with God's power and protection, "All things are possible for him who believes" in God (Mark 9:23); for "Greater is he that is in us than is he that is in the world" (1 John 4:4).

For those who are redeemed and righteous human souls on fire for God, and promote Jesus Christ's gospel message of salvation, "Our daily Bread" issue of October 21st,, 1999, has this to say: (St. Paul speaking in 2 Corinthians 4:16-17),

"Therefore, even though the outward man [or physical body] is perishing [through adversity]... Yet, the inward man [or spirit and soul] is being renewed day by day. [For as we grow more Christ-like, we grow more beautiful, awesome, powerful, spiritual and youthful]; and our light and momentary troubles are achieving for us an eternal glory that far outweighs them all."

Because through Christ Jesus we have been redeemed and have both spiritual and physical freedom, (Galatians 5:1), through Jesus' promise of "abundant life" (John 10:10).

Galatians 5:1 says, "For freedom, Christ has set us free; stand fast therefore, through His mighty power, and do not submit again to a yoke of slavery"—the yoke of Satan's power to afflict and enslave us through sin, with disease, evil, and the fear of death and condemnation to hell-fire for unrighteous living.

Now how can we keep on maintaining our freedom from Satan's yoke of slavery (sin)? Let me tell you how.

We have to be steadfast in the observance and practice of Jesus Christ's self-evident truths recorded in "the Synoptic Gospels"* by His "apostles,"* as well as God's other biblical-truths for righteousness recorded in the Holy Bible. They include all the powerful self-evident truths in the Holy Bible that are real remedies for righteous living, for all the redeemed and the righteous human souls on fire. They also constitute the awesome and holistic powerful values for repentance, deliverance, healing, and freedom from practicing sin, through the power of Christ Jesus—such as the power of prayer, meditation, occasional fasting, and the practice of "agape love,"* along with the blessings of all the other noble celestial gifts of the fruit of the Holy Spirit, which is recorded in Galatians 5:22-23. And also showing compassion for all those who are needy and suffering, with continual praise, worship, and thanksgiving, for God's goodness, His faithfulness, mercy, and grace, mentioned in the Book of Psalms in the Old Testament. We must also exercise our faith in God and ourselves, through Christ Jesus, with a spirit of forgiveness for our enemies. Again, we must pray for all those who persecute us, and have a humble, contrite, and pure heart, leading to our continual daily repentance from sin, which will take us a long way in our Christian journey.

So pray continually about all these powerful spiritual values and virtues, which Jesus taught His disciples about, and try your best to emulate them. For without them, our Christian life's earthly struggles against Satan and his disciples will be powerless, useless, and in vain. I vouch for these truths personally, because in my Christian life and the lives of others, I have seen and proven that these axioms are the answers for all our life's spiritual problems, including the acquisition of God's awesome powers for the redeemed and righteous to perform efficient kingdom ministry.

By now, I hope that you have basically understood or digested my evangelistic outreach Gospel message, about sin and repentance, salvation and eternal life, the power of God's Holy Word and His Holy Spirit for active Kingdom ministry of the redeemed and the righteous human soul or souls on fire, my spiritual identity and journey with Christ Jesus, Jesus's redemptive work for all sinners (including me), on Calvary's wooden cross; and "God's New Dispensation"* of "grace and mercy for us through our faith in Jesus Christ"—for all those who are no longer under the power of God's generational curse for "the Old Dispensation,"* (or "the Ten Commandments" recorded in Exodus 20:1-17), which was given to Moses by God himself, to govern His chosen people Israel of biblical times; and how, when, and why I became a redeemed sinner and righteous human soul on fire for God: "A New Creation,"* which totally defines "who you and I are through Christ Jesus" (2 Corinthians 5:17).

As "a New Creation," my life on earth has been punctuated

by many faith-growths, with many positive healing testimonies of God's loving-kindness to me, through Christ Jesus—including one like Job's in the Holy Bible. These faith-growths which followed my every healing experiences, after God's and Satan's trials and testing, made me stronger and more resolute—especially after God's allowed Satanic afflictions on me, like Job. Eventually, I was so filled with God's grace and mercy, the peace of Christ, and the Holy Spirit's consolation, that I firmly affirmed that, "No weapon formed against me shall prosper." . Just remember, God never gives us more than we can bear, or allows us to be tempted beyond what we can endure. Every redeemed and righteous believer can tell you about his own unique and successful experiences against Satan. As some old creole folk in my country would say in our local language, "Bondye' ca by gal, may e ca by zong pu gwate':" meaning that if God gives you rashes or allows Satan to afflict you with sores (like Job), He will also give you finger-nails to appease or attend to the burning itch that it causes, before it heals. We are all survivors and victors of such a situation in some way, through the power of Christ Jesus who died to redeem or set us free.

So, like these deceased, redeemed, righteous and godly-stalwarts of our Christian faith, I can now boldly affirm:

(a) "No man is ever the same after God has laid His hand upon him" [through Christ Jesus]. (Billy Graham)

(b) "Turn your life over to Jesus Christ today, and your life will never be the same" [again]. (A. W. Tozer)

(c) "The transforming love of God has repositioned me for eternity. I am now a new man, forgiven, basking in the warm love of our living God, trusting His promises and provision, and enjoying life to the fullest" (Bill Bright).

"Our Daily Word" issue of October 22nd, 1984, has this to say about the identity of the redeemed and the righteous:

> "From the depth of my being comes the ringing realization that I am more than I seem; more than the surface self with its lack and pains and limitation. I am a spiritual being, powerful and perfect in God's sight. If ever I feel unable to accomplish all that is before me, I stop a moment and affirm, 'I can, because I have all the strength in me. I have all power in me. I have all light and wisdom and inspiration in me. I can do all things because I am spiritually strong, spiritually powerful, through Christ Jesus who gives me strength' (Philippians 4:13)].
>
> 'I can, because I am.' I think of myself in terms of what I am, not in terms of what I am not. I am the beloved of God. I am all-wise, all-loving, all-conquering child of God. 'I can, because I am.' I meet this day [and every day] centered in God, centered in the 'Truth,' expecting only good. 'I can, because I am.' Nothing daunts me, nothing makes me afraid, nothing keeps me from expressing my Christ self."

To sum up about "WHO ARE YOU AND I THROUGH CHRIST JESUS," 1 Corinthians 2:12 says: "Now we have received not the spirit of the world but the spirit which is from God, [through Christ Jesus], that we might understand the gifts bestowed on us by God."

(a) Therefore, we have now become "New Creations" through Christ Jesus and the Holy Spirit (2 Corinthians 5:17);

(b) We now have the spirit of God in us, and the mind of Christ Jesus; so that we can discern, understand, and explain most spiritual truths; for the Holy Spirit who is also the spirit of God, guides us and teaches us all things (or "all Truths");

(c) We now have special spiritual gifts and powers for, and in our approach to life, for Kingdom ministry: namely, the fruit of the Spirit (Galatians 5:22-23), and the powers of Jesus Christ's Great Commission (Mark 16:15-18; Matthew 28: 18-20);

(d) Consequently, we are no longer controlled by our old self and our selfish habits, or our Adamic nature;

(e) So we release our old self to God, "by letting go and let God rule our life;"

(f) We begin to live for others instead of being self-indulgent: or greedy, envious, covetous, hateful, selfish, jealous, malicious, and prideful. (Matthew 23:25; James 5:15);

(g) And we will no longer have any lack or limitation in our life (Philippians 4:13, 19; Isaiah 58:11; Hebrews 4:6);

(h) God will guide and protect us continually from all evil (Psalms 91, and 121);

(l) His Loving-kindness of grace and mercy will sustain and maintain us continually;

(j) He will be our refuge and strength, and an ever present help in time of trouble (Psalm 46:1);

(k) He will be our "Light" and our "Salvation" (Psalm 27:1-4).

(l) And His Holy Word will be "A Lamp unto our feet and a light to our path" (Psalm 119:105)--and a strength to our life.

"May God be praised!"

4

THE AWESOME POWERS OF ONE REDEEMED OR A RIGHTEOUS HUMAN SOUL ON FIRE FOR GOD

1 Corinthians 4:30, in the NIV Bible, says, "For the Kingdom of God is not a matter of talk, but of POWER: the power of our faith in God and His Holy Word, and in Jesus Christ Gospel message as "the Undiluted Truth of God's Power for humanity's deliverance for Salvation," through the total cleansing, healing, protective, and saving power of Jesus Christ's precious shed blood, the power of Calvary's wooden cross that He carried for our sins, with the awesome power of the Holy Spirit to convict and convince us of our sin (or sins), for us to repent. These awesome powers, as well as the power of one or many redeemed and righteous, born-again human souls on fire for God are incredible. They can save and affect total cleansing, deliverance, protection, and healing, for all fallen humanity. So that by the believer or believers' mentioning of "the powerful name of Jesus," or "the pleading of His precious shed blood," with God's special anointing and outpouring of His grace and mercy on us, or using the power of Jesus Christ's special, efficient, spiritual ministry of "His Great commission," of Mark 16:15-18, miracles happen. All these awesome deliverance spiri-

tual powers for the use of the redeemed and the righteous, for God's kingdom ministry, also include the use of the power of God's Holy Word as a two-edged sword, (called the sword of the Spirit), for Christian defense, healing, and protection, (Hebrews 4:12; Ephesians 6:17, NIV), with the fruit of the Holy Spirit for character building as well (Galatians 5:22-23, NIV). The power of fervent prayer and fasting of a believer, for prayer protection, healing, and deliverance, (James 5:15, NIV), and the use of his powerful, mysterious testimony, with his faith-affirmation in the power of "the blood of the Lamb (Jesus)," also keeps Satan at bay (Revelation 12:11, NIV). It's all about "power!"

Having briefly explained above what the awesome powers of one and many redeemed or righteous human souls on fire for God entails, I will deal with "the powers of one" in greater detail right now, and do the same for "the powers of many," in the following Chapter.

As has been said before in the "General Introduction," the powers of one redeemed or a righteous human soul on fire for God is very unique, exclusive, awesome, very powerful, seemingly strange, sometimes incomprehensive and uncontrollable, inexplicable, uncomfortable, and very humiliating sometimes, but a very rewarding phenomenon. And because most unbelievers and unrighteous persons do not understand that because they are in darkness, and the relationship between knowing and experiencing the power of Christ Jesus and the Holy Spirit, whilst knowing and experiencing the power of God simultaneously is different, as in the New Testament times—as compared to hearing about and getting to know God's power by experiencing Him and the Holy Spirit alone, (as in Old Testament Biblical times), St. Paul said that God's servants and apostles are regarded by the world of unbelievers, (likewise himself), as "Fools for Christ"—or just impressionists and weaklings, or powerless people. And we the redeemed or righteous believers are regarded as "public specta-cles," or worldly show-offs (1 Corinthians 4:1-10).

Whether we have the powers of the redeemed (like St. Paul of the New Testament Biblical era), or the powers of the righteous (like the prophet Elijah of Old Testament Biblical times), it is our faith, love, and hope in the One, True, Living, and merciful God's power within us, (the believers), that matters most. For most sin-cere men of God are driven into kingdom ministry by the power of the Holy Spirit, and their love for and strong faith in the power of God within them. So it is not a matter for faith in God through Jesus Christ alone, as in the New Testament Biblical era. And still, there has never been another or greater and more powerful man of God who walked the earth and was on fire for God, like Our Savior Jesus Christ ("the Lion of Judah")—even though He said in John 14:12-14,

> "I tell you the truth, anyone who has faith in me will do what I have been doing. He will do even greater things than these... And I will do whatever you ask in my name, so that the Son may bring glory to the Father. You may ask me for anything in my name, and I will do it."

Note well: Jesus implied that the redeemed who are righteous will be able to do even greater works than Him, if they have faith in Him—but He was not referring to raising themselves from the dead like he did; He was only referring to His works of ministry to man. I will prove that to you.

What about the Old Testament righteous stalwarts of faith in God who never knew Jesus but performed unbelievable and un-heard of feats in God's name? They did so by the power of God and under the anointing of the Holy Spirit's power. Believe it or not, a wise teacher is one who is many steps ahead of his students, because there is always one or more secrets that he holds back from them—which gives him the edge or special power and recognition over them.

Don't forget that Jesus Christ was not an ordinary man when He walked on earth. He was also God incarnate: He had a dual nature and was therefore also immortal—meaning that He could never die. He had the special power to lay down His life voluntarily, on His own accord, and to take it back. And mortal or natural man, (especially the Jews), did not understand that, when Jesus said to them in John 2:19, "Destroy this temple, and I will raise it again in three days"—Jesus was talking to them about His death, burial, and resurrection of His body.

In John 10:18 of the NIV Bible, Jesus speaks about His life and authority more clearly: "No one takes it [my life] from me, but I lay it down on my own accord. I have the authority to lay it down and the authority to take it up again."

No human being or living soul has ever and can ever accomplish such an amazing feat like this. Only Jesus! Man could and can only achieve today, what is humanly possible, naturally, and what is supernaturally possible through the power of Jesus Christ's "Great Commission," of New Testament Biblical times; and in Old Testament Biblical times, through the power of God and the Holy Spirit—because man is not perfect and immortal like Jesus. Man falls short of God's commandment of love and forgiveness so frequently, that he needs the help of Our Lord and Savior and God's grace and mercy, frequently, to maintain his limited spiritual power; so that he can do all things only through Christ Jesus who strengthens him. So no man has the authority like Jesus Christ to lay down his life and take it back and live again. Not even the prophet Mohammed, Buddha, Confucius, Hari Krishna, or any other ancient biblical-era spiritual men of faith, yesterday or today, have been able to rise from death to live again like Jesus. Jesus died but rose again and still lives and reigns as our king and our

Savior, and is sitting at the right hand side of God's throne in heaven.

Some spiritual men, (just like the prophet Elijah of Old Testament biblical times), have single-handedly performed great, mighty, and seemingly unbelievable miracles like Jesus Christ did, during their kingdom-ministry on earth, but they have not healed all manner of diseases like Jesus did. Some were only able to raise the dead like Jesus, as their greatest feat—like St. Paul in Acts 20:9-12. Elijah stopped the rain and dew from falling for three and a half years, and then caused it to fall again (1 Kings 17); and he miraculously multiplied a small amount of food to feed a widow and her son (1 Kings 17:7-16), but not as many as five thousand people like Jesus (Mark 6:30-44); Moses struck a rock in the desert and caused water to flow from it (Exodus 17:6); and he parted the Red Sea by the power of God, and caused God's once enslaved but liberated people from Egypt (Israel), who were pursued by Pharaoh, to escape completely. And afterwards, by the same power of God, Moses closed back the Red Sea and caused their pursuers to perish (Exodus 14:1-30). Now, here is an incredibly powerful feat like Moses's: Even after death, the dead body of the prophet Elisha, (Elijah's disciple), performed miracles (2 Kings or Sirach 48:12-14). Again, three young godly men were thrown into a fiery furnace by King Nebuchadnezzar, and came out unharmed (Daniel 3:16-28). The prophet Daniel was wrongfully accused and thrown among hungry lions, and by the power of his prayer and faith in Almighty God, he came out unharmed (Daniel 6:7). Elijah prayed to God to send down fire from heaven to consume his sacrificial offering, and God did so; and the pagan priests who worshipped the idol Baal were killed by their own idol worshippers, because Baal could not consume their sacrificial offering(1 King 18:38-40). Job prayed and remained faithful to God in his God sanctioned Satanic-affliction, and afterwards, he was vindicated and healed by God, and rewarded and restored a hundred-fold. All these mentioned phenomena were matters of victory for all God's spiritual stalwarts, because they prayed to Him fervently, and exercised their faith in Him continually. Today, some of these dead spiritual stalwarts are still asleep and waiting (as the Holy Bible puts it), for God's great day of judgement for them to rise from death as everyone else; and they will be judged for the good and bad that they have done in their lifetime, despite their awesome powers as human souls on fire for God.

So when we look at man's life-span on earth, even after having been a powerful human soul on fire for God, the Holy Bible expresses its quality so fittingly by saying:

> "All men [the godly and ungodly] are like grass, [or looking healthy and strong in the beginning], and all their glory [or dominion, power, and majesty] is like the flowers of the field [radiant]; the grass withers and the flowers fall [or they deteriorate and die], but the word of the Lord" [God's eternal presence among men] stands forever [or never disappears] (1 Peter 24-25).

And most important: since God's eternal presence as His Holy Word still preside and resides eternally among men, and the dead grass and flowers of the field becoming earth again seem to be the natural and final destiny of also all the redeemed and righteous who have died, or fade, and disappear from the earth, their powers and presence even in death, still seem to be able to communicate with the living, by even continuing to perform miracles—like the prophet Elisha's corpse did in 2 King, of Holy Scripture For the unrighteous or unbeliever, this scenario seems "far-fetched" or a highly improbable thing and privilege for a corpse, which was once a living, redeemed and righteous human soul on fire for God—but not for the believer, because he or she know that "With God all things are possible (Matthew19:26, NIV). Let me now comment about three special, powerful, righteous, and deceased men of the Old Testament biblical times, and one special redeemed and righteous, deceased man of God of the New Testament era, to show you how God's great and mighty powers worked within them also; so that many unbelievers will come to realize with God all things are possible, and all things are possible to him who believes. It is only a matter of faith in God, and putting that faith into action—just like the old patriarch Abraham did, when God called him from his comfort zone to go to a place or land that he did not know or ever heard about before, and he immediately believed and obeyed God (Genesis 12:1-9). I am referring to Elijah, Elisha, and King David of Old Testament Biblical times, and St. Paul of the New Testament Biblical era, after they were called, chosen, anointed, and sent out by God to do Kingdom ministry, to put their incredible faith in Him into action.

Elijah was an ordinary man like you and me, but with incredible and tremendous faith and power from God; so God gave him an extraordinary and special ministry to undertake. His ministry was so full of drama and powerful feats, that he was called "the fiery prophet"—because his words blazed like a torch, and because he was so bold and fearless sometimes, says Holy Scripture.

The "Good News Bible" says about him, just as in the book of Ecclesiasticus, (or Sirach 48:2-9, like in 1 and 2 Kings of the NKJV Bible).

> "He brought a famine on the people [God's enemies], and many of them died because of his persistence. Speaking in the name of the Lord, he kept the rain from coming, and on three occasions he called down fire [from heaven on God's enemies]. No one else can boast of these deeds... [He also] brought a famous King down to sickness

and death… [And he] was taken up to heaven in a fiery whirlwind, a chariot driven by fiery horses."

He never died a normal or natural death, or was buried like everyone else. Isn't this an awesome power and special privilege or blessing for one righteous human soul on fire for God?

As for the prophet Elisha, Ecclesiasticus of the OKJV or Sirach 48:12-14 of the GNB says about him, as in 2 Kings of NKJV,

> "When Elijah was hidden by the whirl-wind, Elisha [God's prophet] was filled with his spirit [or power]. As long as he [Elisha] lived he was not afraid of rulers, and they could not make him do as they wished. Nothing was too hard for him. Even when he was dead, his body worked miracles."

Could you imagine and believe that awesome power about the corpse of a deceased righteous human soul on fire for God? Amazingly awesome! Even his corpse performed miracles? The Holy Bible says that everything is possible for him who believes in God or Christ Jesus (Mark 9:23; Philippians 4:13, NIV).

Then we have King David, who was a shepherd boy. God chose, anointed, and used him as a powerful soldier of Israel, a skilled musician, a holy man, a very humble and contrite human soul on fire for God, and a man after God's own heart (1 Samuel 13:14). Sirach 47:4-11 says about him:

> "When he was still a boy, he killed a giant [Goliath] to rescue his people [Israel]… so that the nations would have respect for the power of his people [and his God]… The people honored him for killing his tens of thousands, and when he was crowned king, they praised him for being chosen by the Lord. He wiped out all his enemies and per-

manently crushed the Philistines, so that they never again became a threat."

In everything David did, he gave thanks and praise to the Holy Lord, the Most High. He loved his Creator and sang praises to him with all his heart. He put singers at the altar to provide beautiful music. He set the time of the festivals throughout the year and made them splendid occasions; the temple rang with the Lord's praises all day long. The Lord forgave David's sin and established his power forever. He made a covenant with him that he and his descendants would reign in splendor over Israel.

David became a more powerful King of Israel, after his true, sincere, and humble repentance from his sin of murder and adultery—because of God's redeeming love, grace, and mercy. Note well, without perfect contrition for his secret sin of lust, envy, jealousy, and selfishness, as he coveted Uriah's wife before the prophet Nathan exposed him, his secret pride could have easily overtaken a righteous human soul on fire like him, and Satan would have a sure stronghold within him, to destroy his life.

So despite how God uses many righteous and redeemed human souls powerfully to do His kingdom ministry on earth, some human souls on fire sometimes misuse or abuse their powerful spiritual anointing privileges, and become guilty of the worst sinful acts (like King David). Yet, no sin is too great or serious that God can't forgive it—except the sin of blasphemy against God's Holy Spirit. A sinfully defeated human soul on fire for God can easily "bounce back"* through repentance, prayer, and fasting, (like King David), and have a clean slate to face the future. The greater the sin is the more grace (or unconditional favor) and love and mercy God dispenses to the sinful human soul; for His mercy endures forever to all those who fear Him (Psalm 107:1; Luke 1:5). We see this in the life of the Prodigal Son in Luke 15:11-31, and also in the life of St. Paul (a serial killer of Christians), who was redeemed by Jesus Christ, and became a powerfully anointed human soul on fire for God, in the New Testament biblical era.

As a powerful and high-ranking Roman soldier (or official), Paul did not fear God before Jesus Christ and the Holy Spirit arrested him; because he murdered thousands of Christians in the New Testament biblical era. But, when Jesus Christ humbled him through blindness and accusation, and made him fall instantly from his horse, when he was on his way to persecute and kill the Christians in Damascus, he (Paul) came to his senses subsequently, and was converted to Christianity. Afterwards, he became one of the most powerful, diligent, humble, enthusiastic, faithful, long-suffering, and steadfast chosen human souls on fire for God, in the New Testament Christian Church ministry era. So St. Peter says about all God's chosen, anointed, and redeemed human souls on fire for God, (including St. Paul), "But you are a chosen people, a royal priesthood, a holy nation, a people belonging to God, that you may declare the praises of him who has called you out of darkness into his wonderful light" (1 Peter 2:9, NIV).

Paul was in darkness when he was killing and persecuting the Christians, and he did not know that at all; he thought that he was doing the right thing, and was the smartest and wisest person. Likewise, there are many unbelievers and unredeemed persons who are blind and lost in trespasses, or in darkness, and they don't know or have not realized that. Some of them have some worldly power and influence, so they think that they are so mighty and powerful. But, not until they become converted and come to know Jesus Christ as their Lord and Personal Savior, that they come to understand and know the true source of power, and what it is really all about. For real and absolute power comes from God, through Christ Jesus.

The powers that St. Paul had through Christ Jesus after his conversion, was so much greater than the powers of his Roman soldier's office. For he then had supernatural capability to perform all the miraculous works that Jesus Christ assigned his disciples to accomplish through "The Great Commission" (Matthew 28: 18-20, and Mark 16:15-18). Imagine, before Paul's conversion, he had the power to destroy the lives of many Christians and anyone else who was a threat to the Roman establishment; but now, through the power of God, Christ Jesus, and the Holy Spirit within him, he could not only cause God to destroy his enemies at will, but he could also restore, or raise the dead to life and heal the sick. He could also cast out demons, etc. etc. On one occasion Paul was bitten by a poisonous snake, and he just shook it off his hand and did not die. All these powerful phenomena show some of the awesome powers that one redeemed human soul on fire for God has, through the power of God, Christ Jesus, and the Holy Spirit. And every faithful and sincere, Holy Spirit-filled, born-again, redeemed and righteous believer, has and is capable of the same privileges and miraculous works of St. Paul and Jesus. They just have to summon the power of the mustard seed of faith in God within them, through the power of faith in Christ Jesus and the power of the Holy Spirit, and command the mountain or obstacle to be removed, through positive affirmation.

Jesus said in Matthew 17:20 to His disciples, who had such little faith, "I tell you the truth, if you have faith as small as a mustard seed, you can say to this mountain, 'Move from here to there' and it will move. Nothing will be impossible for you."

Because of this experience, St. Paul says in 1 Corinthians 1:18-20, and verse 25,

> "For the message about Christ's death on the cross is nonsense to those who are being lost [those in darkness]; but for us who are being saved it is God's power. The scripture says, 'I will destroy the wisdom of the wise, and set aside the understanding of scholars.' So then where does that leave the wise? or the scholars? ...For what seems to

be God's foolishness is wiser than human wisdom, and what seems to be God's weakness is stronger than human strength."

The spiritual wisdom and power that God gives and reveals to his redeemed and righteous human souls on fire are above and beyond the natural man's understanding. Only the Holy Spirit can open the natural man's eyes, mind, and understanding, to make him see and understand clearly, God's wisdom and truth: an awesome privilege of "truth and power experience," which can only be acquired by a Christ-redeemed, humble, contrite, sincere, and truly repentant sinner, "who lies prostrate at the foot of Calvary's wooden cross" (for want of a better expression).

So Jesus said concerning this experience to His father in heaven, in Matthew 11:25-27, NIV,

> "I praise you Father, Lord of heaven and earth, because you have hidden these things from the wise and the learned, and revealed them to little children [God's child-like, newly redeemed, born-again believers]. Yes Father, for this was your good pleasure. No one knows the Son except the Father, and no one knows the Father except the Son and those to whom the Son chooses to reveal him."

Satan and natural man's spiritual powers and wisdom are no match for and cannot be compared with God's supernatural powers and wisdom through Christ Jesus, for the redeemed and the righteous human souls on fire for Him. For everything in the life of the redeemed or righteous human souls on fire for God, are all about the full and special powerful influences and effects of their awesome, loving, and personal relationship with Jesus Christ, including the supernatural and operational anointing of the Holy Spirit, and the transforming power of God's Holy Word on our heart and mind. This may seem strange or stupid to an unbeliever or an unredeemed person or soul in darkness, for they do not, will not, and cannot understand the secret wisdom and power of the things of light, which is God's hidden wisdom and power.

For example, many unbelievers—and some believers too—do not understand and find it difficult to accept and practice Jesus Christ's spiritual truth principle about forgiveness, which He spoke to St. Peter about, in Matthew 18:21-22, NIV: "I tell you [forgive your delinquent brother or enemy] not seven times, but seventy-seven times." And this also goes for many other teachings of Jesus, such as, "Love your enemies and pray for those who persecute you" (Matthew 5:44, NIV). How do we believers explain these teachings to the unrighteous? Even some of Jesus's disciples, like St. Peter, found it difficult to understand and accept such truth teaching as Matthew 18:21-22, about forgiving a brother seventy-seven times. So now you see why St. Paul says, that the world regards us as "fools for Christ?" Some teachings of Jesus don't seem to make much sense to worldly people. Many persons think we Christians are crazy and stupid when we practice Jesus Christ's truth principles, especially these two mentioned before. But, from my practical experience as a born-again believer, I have proved that Jesus's spiritual truth principles work powerfully, because it helps me maintain my peace of mind. And these are some of the awesome spiritual secrets and godly wisdom that the world does not understand. Only the wisdom, illumination, and power of the Holy Spirit, can help one to understand and accept God's secret truths. And this is a special power and privilege.

To be "spiritually wise," you have to become "a fool for Christ Jesus." And one of the most awesome privileges and powerful results of this experience is the presence of God's supernatural peace and joy that passes all (human) understanding within you, with the wisdom and gentleness of Jesus Christ in your heart and mind. For peace and joy are two of the most powerful spiritual assets of and for every redeemed and righteous believer, when performing kingdom ministry in the world. If it was not so, God's angelic host would not have proclaimed this message to the world at the birth of Jesus Christ. Don't let the Devil steal your peace and joy in ministry; once again, it is your strength, says Nehemiah 8:10.

Next to the powers or assets of peace and joy for the powerful ministry of each redeemed or righteous human soul on fire for God, are the tremendous powers of wisdom and gentleness. They help a believer to quickly discern Satan's evil schemes or tricks. That is why Jesus said to His twelve disciples when He was sending them out into the world to evangelize, "Behold, I send you forth as sheep in the midst of wolves: be ye therefore wise as serpents, and harmless [or gentle and innocent] as doves" (Matthew 10:16, NKJV).

When we analyze the disposition of sheep among a pack of wolves, we see how stupid, naive, helpless, and endangered they are or can be among a pack of wolves, or even dogs. Sheep never seem to observe or sense danger wherever they go or stray. And so, they always put themselves in danger by wandering off into the wrong places or company at the wrong time. Whereas, wolves are very clever, cunning, fierce, calculating, and very wild and unfriendly animals; for they always find themselves at the right places, and at the right time to attack their prey. And they always attack and kill any sheep without shepherd protection, at will. Therefore, Jesus likened the redeemed and righteous unto His sheep in the world, which can be very cruelly victimized by wolves (or the unrighteous persons of this world). Jesus is imploring us therefore, to be as wise (or cautious, cunning, and very calculating) as a serpent, and as gentle as a dove, if we want to survive in God's ministry.

When you know how and when to be observant, cautious, cunning, silent, and calculating as a serpent, then, you will be able to protect yourself from the unbelievers (or wolves), and false Christians, or "wolves in sheep clothing," before they attack and kill you, or take advantage of you. Jesus implied, you must also master the art of being as gentle, innocent, and silent as a dove to protect yourself. When the dove observes that a hunter is very close to it undetected, after having observed him for a while, it suddenly escapes or flies off, startling him. Jesus has asked us to be like a serpent and a dove for one reason: both of them know how to be cunning, to protect themselves, and how to use the element of surprise. So protect yourselves like a dove, and know how and when to attack boldly with the wisdom of a serpent, when proclaiming the gospel message in ministry; and know how to escape or protect yourself like a dove from your attackers, pursuers, or persecutors, when you need to.

After my father had worked in a serpent infested area called Dennery (in St. Lucia, W.I.) for many years, he explained to me that when a serpent is stalking its prey, it is so cunning, clandestine, and calculating, that when you see its eyes are closed it is not sleeping, but just observing its prey carefully and waiting for the prey to reach within its striking distance. And, when its eyes are open, you may think that it is watching you but it is sleeping.

Like Jesus's analogy of the serpent, the dove, and the sheep among wolves, the strategy to have real lasting peace and joy (or true happiness), with wisdom and gentleness for a godly, profitable, and very powerful kingdom ministry, can only be acquired and mastered, by having a personal relationship with Jesus Christ—and not just seeking material riches alone in this life. If God blesses you to have all the riches of "abundant life,"* including a personal relationship with Jesus Christ, then, you have all you need; for you do not have a spirit of greed, envy, lust, and covetousness, but self-denial, contentment, and detachment, from your worldly riches. You have everything necessary for a happy and successful life: spiritual power, peace of heart, soul, and mind, physical and emotional health and strength, protection, joy, wisdom and understanding, patience, humility, longevity, self-control, faith in God, the love of family and friends, and God's unmerited favor of love, grace and mercy. But how can you prevent this complete package of "abundant life" from eluding you, so that Satan will not build a "stronghold"* in you or your life? You must continue to seek God's Kingdom and His righteousness, and all will be well with you.

Don't think that this is an impossible situation, because Jesus came to make it a reality. There is one such example in my family. This year (2021), he will be 101 years old, and God has blessed him throughout his life with good and sound health of mind and body, and enough material wealth. He is one of God's recipients of "abundant life" through Christ Jesus. For Jesus said in John 10:10, NIV, "I have come that they may have life, and have it to the full."

Notwithstanding, let me change my trend of thought here a bit, to explain a few important facts which I mentioned in the opening paragraph of this chapter. It will help you to further understand "The Awesome Powers of One Redeemed or Righteous Human Soul on Fire for God."

Firstly, one must also be very mindful, that when one redeemed or righteous human soul is on fire for God, and is operating under the powerful and awesome anointing of the Holy Spirit, the power of God's grace and mercy, and the amazing coveted power of being under and protected by Jesus Christ's shed precious blood, his or her powers are unique and very exclusive—because God, Jesus Christ and the Holy Spirit, cannot dwell in an unclean body, to do kingdom ministry. Therefore, one must do plenty of soul searching, prayer and fasting, and study and meditation on God's Holy Word day and night—as preparation, so that he or she can become acceptable for God's to use (Psalm 1:1-2).

Secondly, the redeemed and the righteous powers are very strange, and they move unpredictably like the wind. For example, like speaking in tongues. This phenomenon can also be a bit humiliating and overwhelming sometimes, because it is not easy to control and predict how, when, and where the spirit of God and the Holy Spirit's power will move and/or work in a believer. And since God's ways are not like men's ways, and He is always in control, God always calls the shots by deciding what powers of anointing a believer should have for His kingdom ministry. We see and observe all these trends and patterns even for and in deliverance services: some believers are spiritual healers of the sick, while some others specialize in casting out demons, prophesying, and/or raising the dead, or healing the effects or causes of spiritual wickedness in high places, etc. And sometimes God gives most of these gifts of deliverance to some particular believers who sincerely imitate Christ, (as in the New Testament Church biblical times); so that God can receive even greater glory through their faith in the awesome power of Jesus Christ. For Jesus Christ is the answer to every human problem. He is the greatest physician, the physician of all physicians, and the greatest example of the awesome powers of one human soul on fire for God. The greater the gift or the more talents that God gives to you for ministry, it is the more He expects of or from you. So be careful what you sow; you may not like the harvest if you sow bad seed.

Therefore, all God's servants, (such as the bishops, elders, pastors, deacons, priests, ministers, evangelists, apostles, and the laity), who have been redeemed and are in ministry for God through the power of Christ Jesus, have to be very careful about the power and anointing that God has vested in them for service—especially when success and popularity begin to loom up its deceptive head in their corner. Satan has a way of building strongholds of pride, greed, envy, jealousy, hatred, covetousness, and arrogance in their minds and hearts, with a desire for fame and riches—so that humility, patience, longsuffering, selflessness, self-denial, Godly wisdom, faith in God, a spirit of forgiveness, compassion, agape love, and self-control, finally go out of the window. And God's servants soon become like tasteless salt, or lukewarm, pseudo-redeemed, unrighteous human souls, who have no more zeal and fire for Jesus anymore, but only for personal financial interests and gain in kingdom ministry. Well, what does Jesus say in Revelation 3:15-22 in the NIV Bible, about that situation in the church of Laodicea?

> "I know your deeds, that you are neither cold nor hot. I wish you were either one or the other! So, because you are lukewarm—neither hot nor cold—I am about to spit you out of my mouth. You say, 'I am rich; I have acquired wealth and do not need a thing.' But you do not realize that you are wretched, pitiful, poor, blind, and naked. I council you to buy from me gold refined in the fire, so you can become rich; and white clothes to wear, so that you can cover your shameful nakedness; and salve to put on your eyes, so you can see.
>
> Those whom I love I rebuke and discipline. So be earnest and repent. Here I am! I stand at the door and knock. If anyone hears my voice and opens the door, I will come in and eat with him, and he with me.
>
> To him who overcomes, I will give the right to sit with me on my throne, just as I overcame and sat with my Father on his throne. He who has an ear, let him hear what the Spirit [of Christ Jesus] says to the Churches."

God's spiritual gifts of power are never to edify ourselves on earth, but to enhance and promote His kingdom ministry; so that we become His vessels of honor and glory for performing mighty works like Christ Jesus, only after being redeemed and commissioned by Jesus, to give Him (God) all the praise, honor, and glory, that He rightly deserves.

When I observe some elite servants of God today, I notice that some of them have the attitude of Simon (the converted Samaritan sorcerer in Acts 8:18-19), who coveted St. Peter's powerful spiritual gifts from God, with the intention of using it to become wealthy, and to gain personal glory and fame. Most of them claim to have, or if not covet, all the spiritual gift of Jesus Christ, for the sake of trying to achieve prosperity in ministry. But we all know that God does not give all His redeemed and righteous servants the same amount of talents (or gifts) for His kingdom ministry. And that these gifts of power are priceless, very unique, exclusive, and can neither be bought nor sold.

Consequently, I must emphasize here that a redeemed and righteous servant of God must always focus on and live specially for Jesus Christ alone, by denying himself and die to selfishness and sin. And, he must be Holy Spirit-filled, faith-filled, very prayerful, humble, compassionate, patient, and, most importantly, obedient to God's Holy Word through faithfulness to Jesus Christ's teachings. For Jesus Christ alone can keep him safe and empowered always. Jesus will protect, cleanse, and deliver him/her, from the sinful spirits of pride, arrogance, greed, and other evil desires, including the Satanic, negative and harmful reminders of his guilty past and present feelings, to give him a free and gloriously anointed future on earth, and in the hereafter. The power of Jesus Christ is specially the power that he/she needs to overcome Satan and his evil schemes; for Satan and his demons even tremble at the mention of "His name." His name is "awesome power" for the believer, or one redeemed or righteous human soul on fire for God.

"Our Daily Bread" issue of August 7th, 1988, said, "One step in obedience [to Christ] is worth years of study about Him."

Let me now quote a passage in Holy Scripture from Ecclesiasticus 2:1-9, in the Old King James Version Bible, using its modern version in the GNB Bible, about the attitudes of patience, obedience, and faithfulness, which a redeemed or righteous servant of God should have in kingdom service, to conquer Satan and his cohorts through Christ Jesus.

> "Son, if you are going to serve the Lord, be prepared for times when you will be put to the test [through humiliation especially]. Be sincere and determined. Keep calm when trouble comes. Stay with the Lord; never abandon him, [be faithful], and you will be prosperous at the end of your days. Accept whatever happens to you. Even if you suffer humiliation, be patient. Trust the Lord and he will help you. Walk straight in his ways, and put your hope in him.
>
> All you that fear the Lord, wait for him to show you his mercy. Do not turn away from him, or you will fall. All you that fear the Lord, trust him and you will certainly be rewarded. All you that fear the Lord, look forward to his blessings of mercy and eternal happiness."

I reiterate, just be humble, patient, faithful, prayerful, and obedient to Almighty God, during your trials, temptations, and storms of life in Kingdom ministry. You will be victorious in the end, for God will see you through it all, and He will not withhold any good thing from you—including His powerful spiritual gifts and rewards for kingdom ministry. I am a living testimony of these fore-mentioned experiences.

Like Job in the holy Bible, I never gave up on God's faithfulness and His promises for and to all believers. God allowed Satan to afflict and humble me in my youth, for many years. But He finally delivered me and made me prosperous again in my latter years. This proves that God is faithful, and a rewarder of all those who diligently seek Him faithfully, especially His redeemed and righteous servants who are on fire for Him—even though He allows bad things to happen to good people. So I quote here two verses of my favorite Psalm in the Holy Bible: Psalm 34, verses 19 and 22, NKJV, as another testimony of mine about the powers and privileges of one redeemed or a righteous human soul on fire for God. It reads: "Many are the afflictions of the righteous; but the Lord delivereth him out of them all [not some, all!]... The Lord redeemeth the soul of his servants; and none of them that trusteth in him shall be desolate." (The redeemed souls face the same experience).

I have been humiliated often, sometimes discouraged, persecuted, ridiculed, scorned, rejected, neglected, ignored, tried, tested, and frequently scourged by the malicious tongues of false friends, enemies, gossipers, and backbiters—just to remind me of my dark past, including my failures and mistakes; but I never gave up on God, Jesus, and the Holy Spirit, in my Christian life-struggles. My faith in the Holy Trinity has kept me focused and steadfast on the way of salvation and righteousness.

Let's face the naked-truth: who in this life does not have a dark past experience, history, or hidden skeletons in his or her closet? And he or she would not want or like it exposed or talked about or be reminded of? Nobody! Notwithstanding, only a bornagain, redeemed or righteous believer in Christ Jesus, will not be ashamed and fearful to revisit such a past; for he or she does not fear the Satanic, emotional, and disastrous or harmful consequences of it.

For, 1 John 4:4, in the NIV, says, "Greater is he [Jesus] that is in him [the human soul on fire], than he [Satan] that is in the world."

And Jesus said in Luke 10:19, NIV, "I have given you authority [power] to tread on snakes and scorpions and to overcome all the powers of the enemy; nothing will harm you."

Therefore, Isaiah 54:17 says, in the NIV, "....No weapon forged against you will prevail, and you will refute every tongue that accuses you. This is the heritage of the servants of the Lord, and this is their vindication from me, declares the Lord."

So the redeemed or righteous soul feels duty-bound and comfortable with and about revisiting or talking about his past ("with no reservations"), in the form of what he calls "his testimony." For it is "his testimony-giving-power" that helps to strengthen, encourage, save, and bless other believers and unbelievers, who are struggling with the same or similar life-problems that he had: meaning that, if God can deliver, save, cleanse, and transform and reform to make a wretched soul like him whole, free, and respectable again, (through the power of Christ Jesus), He can do it for you and others too—including those who are already messed-up.

Testimony giving is simply telling other persons (or people) about your deliverance and salvation gift from God, through His undeserved grace and mercy for all repentant sinners, and the power of Christ Jesus to save us: how God miraculously delivered you from your sin or your problematic situation, through the awesome saving power of Jesus Christ's shed blood on Calvary's cross, and Holy Spirit conviction.

The testimony giving power of one redeemed or righteous human soul on fire for God, can completely free from sin or deliver and save, (through the power of Christ Jesus and the Holy Spirit's conviction,), thousands of lost or already condemned human souls in a few minutes. And Satan knows that very well! Therefore, he specially hates Christian open-air camp meetings and crusades, physically or via media.

Satan uses fear and discouragement tactics to prevent all the redeemed and the righteous human souls on fire from giving their testimony about God's power and goodness, after they have confessed their sin or sins and were forgiven, through the dispensation of God's prolific grace and mercy in Christ Jesus.

Satan and his worldly disciples are afraid of the testimony of the redeemed, born-again believer, because he (the believer) candidly, contritely, and boldly reveals the truth about his own dark and shameful past, and exposes and blames Satan for the dark, clandestine, sinister, and closeted wicked deeds of evil men.

So when a testimony is given by the redeemed or the righteous, Satan and his disciples feel themselves literally targeted, observed, exposed, seen, ridiculed, and very embarrassed, like disturbed termites coming out of a hidden woodwork or a dark closet—as though and because their evil deeds have come out and back to haunt them. And all they immediately begin to experience is blame, hatred, shame, fear, confusion, condemnation, defeat, and God's judgement. As the saying goes, "If you cannot beat them you must join them." So after Satan's convicted evil disciples hear the testimony of the redeemed or righteous, they have no other choice but to examine themselves and acknowledge and confess their sin (or sins), with shame and humility, and surrender their life to God because of Holy Spirit's conviction.

The matchless, mysterious, convicting, and arresting power of the Holy Spirit and Christ Jesus, through a believer's testimony giving is extremely important, powerful, and awesome. Satan's disciples experience total defeat; and they finally join the redeemed and the righteous to fight for the kingdom of God. Whether you believe it or not, the Holy Spirit and Christ Jesus are powerful allies: their united power in a born-again redeemed-believer's testimony is exclusively one of the most positive and powerful weapons for God's conquest of Satan's kingdom. So once more I remind the redeemed and the righteous human souls on fire for God to be courageous in their Christian struggles and battles, and continue to overcome Satan and his disciples, "by the blood of the Lamb [Jesus], and the word of their testimony" (Revelation 12:11).

THERE IS TREMENDOUS POWER IN ONE REDEEMED OR RIGHTEOUS HUMAN SOUL ON FIRE FOR GOD, BECAUSE OF HIS OR HER REGULAR PLEADING OF THE MIGHTY POWERS OF JESUS CHRIST'S PRECIOUS BLOOD AND NAME, IN ALL ADVERSE SITUA-TIONS, AND HIS/HER EVER-READY HOLY SPIRIT AND FAITH-FILLED TESTIMONY.

Therefore, a redeemed or righteous human soul on fire for God should not worry about what people say or think about him or her, especially when he is doing ministry for God, through Christ Jesus. For the natural man does not and cannot understand the power of supernatural phenomena. So expect any sarcastic or de-grading remarks from him, because he is spiritually blind.

In 1 Corinthians 2:14, in the NIV Bible, St. Paul says,

> "The man without the spirit does not accept the things that come from the Spirit of God, for they are foolishness to him, and he cannot understand them, because they are spiritually discerned. The spiritual man makes judgement about all things, but he himself is not subject to any man's judgements."

So as a believer, when you have some leisure time, please read about the exploits of God's Old Testament righteous persons who were on fire for Him, as well as the New Testament Christian stalwarts like St. Paul, St. Peter, and St. Stephen, whom I have al-ready mentioned.

Observe how St. Paul was feared even more by unbelievers than Christians, after he became converted or a redeemed, born-again human soul on fire for God—all because he now had more special powers through Christ Jesus. What they did not understand was that this wicked man (Paul) who once had earthly powers to pursue and kill Christians was now being pursued by his own, past wicked cohorts and other associates, and was now harmless to them. And that he became Satan's public enemy number 1; because he could no longer continue to destroy God's people. Jesus Christ and God's Holy Spirit arrested him, and he had to join the Christian battle against Satan and his cohorts. I know that some Christians have had or are now going through that same experience like St. Paul.

Paul preached the Gospel message of Jesus Christ for many years in "Asia Minor,"* and he was imprisoned for it many times. He was also shipwrecked, escaped being eaten by wild animals, persecuted, ridiculed, scorned, and escaped many enemy attempts on his life, but he still pressed on diligently and powerfully in God's ministry, through the power of Christ Jesus. He was finally martyred (later on) in Rome, in 67 AD, and was considered as one of the most powerful human souls on fire for God, in the New Testament Christianity era.

Before St. Paul's "conversion,"* he was a high ranking Roman official; and he also gave orders for and witnessed that St. Stephen be stoned to death. Then, after St. Stephen's death, God made Paul suffer the same terrible fate of persecution that he had put many Christians through, for preaching and witnessing to the Gospel message of Jesus Christ. And despite all of that, St. Paul's mind, heart, and spirit was very persistent, and resolutely on fire for Jesus. For, even from the prisons where he was occasionally incarcerated and regularly whipped, he still proclaimed the Gospel and witnessed for Jesus: he wrote many consoling, encouraging, and powerful theological letters (or epistles, as it is sometimes called), to and for the many problematic Christian churches in Asia Minor.

Saving souls for Christ Jesus was his passion, especially "the

Gentiles."* Therefore, when he was on fire for God, through the power of Christ Jesus and the Holy Spirit, he was nick-named and known in the Christian world as, "the apostle to and for the Gentiles." Likewise, all human souls on fire for God in Asia Minor who lived like Jesus, were called "Christians"*--pre-supposing that they also had a personal encounter with Jesus Christ.

Modern day presenters of special Christian stalwarts who are examples of the power of one human soul on fire for God, have not failed to recognize and mention evangelist Billy Graham, Benny Hinn, (a healer), Bishop T. D. Jakes, and a humble, gentle, powerful, and a recently deceased human soul on fire for God in India, like Mother Teresa of Calcutta. She was a Roman Catholic nun who worked tirelessly and feverishly to alleviate poverty, hunger and disease, in the slums and streets of India. And although she was not as spiritually gifted like St. Paul, or the prophets Isaiah, Elijah, or Elisha, etc. , those who knew her said that she was a powerful human soul on fire for God, through her "Agape Love."* Her love and compassion for the poor and the destitute in India went hand in hand with Jesus Christ's teaching in Matthew 25:31-46. So undoubtedly, she knew Jesus and had a personal encounter and relationship with Him.

Therefore, on page 20 in the book "Light for My Path," Mother Teresa is quoted as having said, "The biggest disease today is not leprosy or tuberculosis [as in past times], but rather the feeling of being unwanted, uncared for, and deserted by everybody. [And] The greatest evil is the lack of love and charity."

Or, just putting it in another way: the lack of the power of true Christian love and compassion for and among the poor and the destitute in India. As Jesus Christ said in Matthew, Chapter 25 and verse 40, about true Christian love and compassion, "Whatever you did for one of the least of these brothers of mine, you did for me." For "Faith without works is dead," says the letter of James, in Chapter 2, verse 26. This phenomenon will also be part of God's criteria for our salvation and eternal life on "judgment day,"* when the Son of Man (Jesus) will come again in all His power and heavenly glory, with all His angels, to judge all the living and the dead (Matthew 25:31-46).

There are many other deceased Christian stalwarts from many different countries and other religious faiths, who have left behind many powerful legacies and memories of their exceptional power of selfless, unconditional, and compassionate Christian love for Jesus and all humanity to emulate—after God called and anointed them for their earthly ministry: like D. L. Moody, C. H. Splurgon, Pope John the XX111, Martin Luther (the German Catholic monk and reformer), Rev. Dr. Martin Luther King, etc., etc. I wish you would dare to observe and emulate their contribution, by nurturing their humility, patience, faith in God, courage, dedication, faithfulness, enthusiasm, Godly wisdom, love, peace of heart and mind, self-control, and the spirit of forgiveness for all their enemies. Their life stories are powerful testimonies

And among all the many spiritual stalwarts who have made their special contribution to humanity, as powerful human souls on fire for God, some have passed on or are deceased. But, we must not forget the greatest and most powerfully anointed one of all: JESUS CHRIST himself: The One who died, was risen, and is still alive and well today. He is sitting now also on the right hand side of God's throne interceding for us, when we sin again or have a petition, after being saved. He deserves all the honor, praise, and glory from us, because He is OUR GREAT INTERCESSOR (Romans 8:34); OUR GREAT HIGH PRIEST (Hebrews 7:1); THE KING OF KINGS AND LORD OF LORDS (Revelations 17:14); THE LORD OF HEAVEN AND EARTH; THE GREAT PHYSICIAN (Matthew 23:16); THE GREAT TEACHER (John 3:2); OUR WONDERFUL COUNSELLOR (Isaiah 9:6); THE PRINCE OF PEACE (Isaiah 9:6); THE AUTHOR AND FINISHER OF OUR CHRISTIAN FAITH (Hebrews 12:6); THE MOST RENOWNED, COMPASSIONATE, AND MERCIFUL SOUL WHO

WALKED THE EARTH; OUR SAVIOR, OR THE LAMB OF GOD WHO TAKES AWAY THE SINS OF THE WORLD (John 4:42); THE WORD MADE FLESH AND DWELLED AMONG US (John 1:1); THE WAY, TRUTH, AND LIFE (John 14:6); THE ONLY WAY TO THE FATHER (GOD) IN HEAVEN (John 14:6); THE ONLY ANSWER TO AND FOR ALL MAN'S PROBLEMS; THE CONQUERING LION OF THE TRIBE OF JUDAH (Revelation 5:5); THE ALPHA AND THE OMEGA, or the beginning and the end (Revelation 22:13); OUR SOON COMING KING (Revelations 22:12); OUR KING (Revelations 7:17); OUR SHEPHERD (Revelation 7:17); THE KING OF GLORY (Psalm 24:7); THE SACRIFICIAL AND VICTORIOUS LAMB (Revelations 5:6-14); THE GREAT "I AM" like God Himself (Revelations 22:13); THE BREAD OF LIFE (John 6:25-59); OUR REDEEMER (Revelation 7:14); THE LIGHTOF THE WORLD (John 8:12); THE TRUE VINE (John 15:1); and OUR ONLY SOURCE OF GOD'S COMPLETE PACKAGE FOR "ABUNDANT LIFE" (John 10:10). Humanity needs Him and His teachings and answers now more than ever. Try Him and you will not regret His answers or solutions for your problems, and the power of His love and forgiveness. No sin is too great or too severe that He will not or cannot handle or intercede with God to forgive you. For He is the most trustworthy and faithful friend that anyone could have: a friend in deed; someone that anyone can rely on. One who can do exceedingly, abundantly, above all, or even more than you can imagine. And He will love you and stick to you closer than a brother; His love never fails! He does not only embody all the awesome powers of one godly human soul on fire, but the collective awesome powers of many human souls on fire for God. So let's give Him all the thanksgiving, honor, praise, and glory, that He truly and rightly deserves—as the most powerful human soul on fire for God.

5

THE AWESOME POWERS OF MANY REDEEMED AND RIGHTEOUS HUMAN SOULS ON FIRE FOR GOD

The awesome powers of many redeemed and righteous human souls on fire for God can be better represented, (or shown), by the powerful collective results of the united prayers and witnessing action, of many faith-filled, humble, bold, wise, and anointed believers on fire for God, in one accord, on Pentecost Sunday (Acts 2). Such a phenomenon was the effect and result of the operational powers of the Holy Spirit, after these believers had already been called, chosen, and anointed, for Kingdom ministry. And their godly duties were to come together, work together, and stay together in one accord, as a righteous body, (even in adversity), to do God's kingdom ministry on earth—as in Acts 2:1-13, in the Holy Bible. Believe it or not, these Holy Spirit awesomely bestowed spiritual powers on Jesus' Apostles and disciples, on Pentecost Sunday, are still available for today's believers. And they are the most powerful spiritual tools that the redeemed and righteous believers have to use, and are still using presently, to do God's supernatural kingdom ministry on earth—as a spiritually united body called "God's Church."*

Biblically speaking, the natural man can only achieve ordinary or natural things in ministry; but with God's help or supernatural powers, he can do extraordinary and supernatural works and miracles; because with God all things are possible. So for "God's Church" to survive and prevail on earth against Satan and the gates of hell, man must operate only with supernatural powers; for Satan is a powerful supernatural being and foe. Thus, the Holy Bible states categorically, that man must operate God's Church on earth as follows:

(a) Not by human might, nor by natural power, but by God's spirit, says the Lord Almighty (Zachariah 4:6, NIV).

(b) For, "It is not I," says Jesus, [just as all human souls on fire in one accord should say], "but the Father [God] who dwells within me [or us believers] who does his work." (John 14:10)

(c) And because "God did not give us [the redeemed and the righteous] a spirit of timidity [fear], but a spirit of power [supernatural power], of love [agape' love], and self-discipline [or self-control, or a sound mind]," believers should realize, as 2 Timothy 1:7 says, "In him we live and move, and have our being" (Acts 17:28, NKJV).

There is sufficient evidence to support these above quoted facts in Chapter 2 of the book of Acts, in the Holy Bible. By the power of God's Holy Spirit, Jesus's twelve apostles and some of His disciples, prayed fervently in strange tongues, and then witnessed to the unconverted Pentecostal crowd, following which a miracle happened. Particularly speaking, it was the apostles of

Jesus, including St. Peter especially, who witnessed and spoke in strange tongues called "Glossolalia," to the unconverted Pentecostal crowd, and three thousand souls were saved that day. For each different nationality present in the Pentecostal crowd heard "the Good News of Jesus Christ's gospel message," in their own native language (Acts 2:4).

Consequently, those who were saved through Peter's preaching by the power of the Holy Spirit, and the disciples witnessing, were amazed, convinced, and convicted in their consciences; so they gladly received the gospel message and water baptism. As said before, Holy Scripture says in Acts 2:41, that about 3,000 human souls were added to the number of believers that day. This was the first spectacular occurrence of evangelism by or through Christian witnessing, in the history of Christendom. And such a tremendous manifestation and exhibition of the Holy Spirit's unique and awesome power on earth, was particularly because of ITS first-time-indwelling and mysterious presence, amongst believers.

Remember: The fear-stricken, redeemed apostles and some believers in Christ Jesus, who previously isolated and hid themselves in an upper room, (after Jesus Christ's crucifixion, death, and resurrection), eventually and finally became Holy Spirit-filled with boldness, awesome power, and faith in Jesus Christ. They were now so very self-confident and bold, that they established the first Christian Church based on their "Apostolic faith."* All this happened on Pentecost Sunday.

So from Pentecost Sunday onwards, the first Church of Jesus Christ based on the apostles' faith in Him and His teaching, began to grow, spread, and prosper, in many countries in Asia Minor, by the power of the Holy Spirit. Finally, the believers in the Church of Jesus Christ at Antioch were first called Christians, because they lived a Christ-like life. And until today, Satan and the gates of hell have not prevailed against God's established Churches by the Apostles; because, as Jesus Christ said in John 5:17, NIV, "My Father is always at work to this very day, and I, too, am working,"

Even though Satan himself never rests or sleeps, and is always at work trying to destroy believers of God's Church.

Apart from God's work and the Holy Spirit's vigilance, and with Jesus Christ's supernatural work in heaven and on earth, the awesome supernatural effects of the powerful prayers of God's united and anointed body of redeemed and righteous believers on earth called God's Church, has still survived—all because of the believers' use of the powers of "Jesus Christ's precious blood" and "His mighty name," as well as the powers of "His Great Commission" for His disciples for Kingdom ministry, in Matthew 28:18-20 and Mark 16:15-18. The use of the fruit of the Holy Spirit for character building within faithful believers, and their powerful testimonies, have also made a great impact and contribution: together, they have helped God's Churches' militants to sustain, maintain, preserve, and promote, all His established Churches on earth. Therefore, God's Churches on earth are not fighting a losing battle; they have complete victory over Satan and his cohorts through the power of their faith in Christ Jesus, and the Holy Spirit.

1 John 5:4 of the NKJV Bible says, "For whatsoever is born of God overcometh the world [Satan and his disciples' schemes]; and this is the victory that overcometh the world, even our faith."

So that is why Jesus said to His disciples before commissioning them for service, in Matthew 28:18, NKJV, "All power is given to me in heaven and in earth."

And to St. Peter (who was the first head and representative for God's Church militants on earth), He said, "I will build my church, and the gates of Hades [hell] will not overcome it" (Matthew 16:18, NIV). "[For] I will give you [Peter] the keys of the kingdom of heaven, [a symbol of power and authority]; whatever you bind on earth will be bound in heaven, and whatever you loose on earth will be loosed in heaven" (Matthew 16:19, NIV).

Knowing that, St. Paul's joy as a disciple of Jesus Christ was so full and complete, that he said to the Church militants of Philippi in Asia Minor:

> "I thank my God every time I remember you. In all my prayers for all of you, I always pray with joy because of your partnership in the gospel from the first day until now, being confident of this, that he who began a good work in you will carry it unto completion until the day of Christ" [Judgment Day] (Philippians 1:3-6, NIV).

So one of the greatest consolations for the redeemed and the righteous Church militants whilst they evangelize as human souls on fire for God, are Jesus' words in Matthew 28, verse 20: "And surely, I am with you always, to the very end of the age "—meaning now, and until the end of time: a very positive and consoling assurance indeed!

This is the greatest and final result and test of the diligent use of the awesome powers and work of the many redeemed and righteous human souls on fire for God's Church on earth, through the specially credited supernatural powers for the ministry of "The Powerful Name" and "The Powerful Precious Blood of Jesus," and the use of the amazing supernatural power and fruit of the Holy Spirit, which was first bestowed on Christ's apostles and many believers from Pentecost Sunday—not forgetting of course the power of God's Holy Word, which Christians use as a two-edged sword in battle against Satan and his disciples, and the powerful faith-filled and fervent prayers and testimony of the redeemed and righteous. May God be praised, worshiped, blessed, and glorified, for all the Blessed Trinity's work, and the awesome powers that "They" gave and still give to all the redeemed and righteous human souls on fire, for God's Kingdom ministry.

6

SOME OF GOD'S MOST POWERFUL BIBLICAL PROMISES FOR "ABUNDANT LIFE," FOR ALL THE REDEEMED AND THE RIGHTEOUS HUMAN SOULS ON FIRE FOR HIM

INTRODUCTION

God did not save us through Christ Jesus, for us to become dormant or lukewarm Christians. He did so, so that all His powerful biblical promises with positive assurances can be work incentives, for all the redeemed and the righteous to strive for salvation and eternal life rewards. And these biblical promises with positive assurances are strictly and particularly based on our righteous character, through the fruit of the Holy Spirit within us; so that the Holy Spirit's power and boldness for our Kingdom ministry of selfless-love, compassion, joy, peace, patience, faithfulness, self-control, humility, and godly faith, could be openly demonstrated. The whole Bible is full of such exemplary men and women, who we should try to emulate. And surely, their righteousness and boldness would not have manifested itself to God and the world, or even influence God's positive assurances and results for them, until either God or Jesus Christ became Lord, Master, and Ruler of their lives, and the Holy Spirit had prompted them to fiery, faith-filled action, for and in God's kingdom ministry.

The term "positive assurances" above, strictly refers to God's sure and righteous commitment to be faithful and true to us, with His visibly positive results as rewards, for all those who are right-eous and redeemed; so that all men can marvel in awe and won-der at His power and faithfulness, and give Him all the honor, thanks, praise, glory and worship, that He rightly deserves—as our loving Father, our Creator, Provider, Protector, Refuge in times of trouble, our Strength, Light, Salvation, Justifier, Deliverer, Shep-herd, Healer, Source of righteousness, Sanctifier, and our Source of peace and freedom.

And whereas the term "the redeemed" refers to a sinner who has been "saved" by his repentance from sin, and the price that Jesus Christ paid for our sins on the cross of Calvary, and he prac-tices a living faith and obedience to God through Christ Jesus, the phrase "God's powerful biblical promises with positive assurances for the redeemed and righteous," refers to "the rewards of right-eous living." And, when we talk about "righteous living," we are referring to God's package of and for "holy living," which Jesus Christ clearly made reference to in John 10:9-11, as "an abundant-life-situation."

For Jesus Christ said in John 10:10, NIV,

> "The thief [Satan] comes only to steal and kill and destroy; I am come that they [all believers: the redeemed and the righteous] may have life [salvation and eternal life through deliverance from sin], and have it to the full" [complete prosperity: spiritual, emotional, financial, intellectual, and physical deliverance].

During the act of holy or righteous living, God has promised to supply all our needs—"Abundant life," or "Life to the full" through Christ Jesus—and to take back all what the devil has stolen from you and me, through the invincible power of Christ Jesus (Philippians 4:19, NIV).

Let me now list below with biblical references, some of God's "life to the full" promised-assurance issues that Jesus Christ and some holy men of stalwart faith and hope experienced, and had to deal with in past biblical times. For God has promised through our faith in Him through Christ Jesus, to supply all our needs for "Abundant Life." And His promise was not only meant for past biblical times alone, but also for today and the future. With patience, wisdom, understanding, practical experience, and self-control, we will come to realize that not everything that we want is necessarily good for us, but only what we need to live a holy or righteous life.

IN GOD'S MOST POWERFUL BIBLICAL PROMISES FOR "ABUNDANT LIFE," FOR ALL THE REDEEMED AND THE RIGHTEOUS HUMAN SOULS ON FIRE FOR HIM, HE PROMISES US:

1. OUR BASIC NEEDS OF: Food, shelter, and clothing, among others. King David positively attests to these issues for us in Psalms 23:1; Psalm 34:10; and Psalm 37:25. And most important, listen to what Jesus Christ said about God's provision for our daily needs, in Matthew 6:26-34:

> "Look at the birds of the air; they do not sow nor reap or stow away in barns, and yet your heavenly Father feeds them. Are you not more valuable than they? Who of you by worrying can add a single hour to his life? ... So do not worry saying, 'What shall we eat?' or 'What shall we drink?' or 'What shall we wear?' For the pagans run after

all these things. And your heavenly father knows that you need them. But seek first his Kingdom and his righteousness [holy living], and all these things will be given to you as well. Therefore do not worry about tomorrow, for tomorrow will worry about itself. Each day has enough troubles of its own."

So, as the old saying goes: "Do not cross a bridge before you reach it! Live one day at a time."

2. THE ASSURANCE OF CONFIDENCE, COMFORT, AND COURAGE, DURING ADVERSITY: King David attests to this by saying,

> (a) "The Lord is my light and my salvation—whom shall I fear? The Lord is the strong-hold of my life—of whom shall I be afraid? When evil men advance against me to devour my flesh, when my enemies and foes attack me, they will stumble and fall. Though an army besiege me my heart will not fear; though war break out against me, even then will I be confident" (Psalm 27:1-3, NIV).

> (b) "Even though I walk through the valley of the shadow of death, I will fear no evil, for you [Jesus the Great Shepherd] are with me; your rod and your staff they comfort me" (Psalm 23:4, NIV).

> (c) So, "Be strong and courageous. Do not be terrified; do not be discouraged, for the Lord your God will be with you wherever you go," says Joshua 1:9, NIV.

3. PROTECTION AND DELIVERANCE FROM THE EVIL-ONE, AND OUR ENEMIES:

(a) "If you make the Most High your dwelling... no harm will befall you, no disaster will come near your tent. For he will command his angels concerning you to guard you in all your ways; they will lift you up in their hands, so that you will not strike your foot against a stone... 'Because he loves me,' says the Lord, 'I will rescue him; I will protect him, for he acknowledges my name. He will call upon me, and I will answer him; I will be with him in trouble, I will deliver him and honor him. With long life I will satisfy him and show him my salvation'" (Psalm 91:9-16, NIV).

(b) "Surely he [God] will save you from the fowler's snare and from the deadly pestilence" (Psalm 91:3, NIV).

(c) "A thousand may fall at your side, ten thousand at your right hand, but it will not come near you. You will only observe with your eyes and see the punishment of the wicked" (Psalm 91:7-8, NIV).

(d) For, "The Lord is my [your] light and my salvation... When evil men advance against me [you] to devour my [your] flesh, when my [your] enemies and my [your] foes attack me [you], they will stumble and fall" (Psalm 27:1-2, NIV).

(e) "The Lord will keep you from all harm—he will watch over your life; the Lord will watch over your coming and going both now and forevermore" (Psalm 121:7-8, NIV).

(f) "No weapon forged against you shall prevail, and you will refute every tongue that accuses you. This is the heritage of the servants of the Lord, and this is their vindication from me," says the Lord. (Isaiah 54: 17, NIV)

(g) "I will strengthen you and help you; I will uphold you with my righteous hand. All who rage against you will surely be ashamed and disgraced; those who oppose you will be as nothing and perish," says the Lord. (Isaiah 41:10-11, NIV)

4. BE OUR SHEPHERD:

(a) "Know that the Lord is God. It is he who made us and we are his; we are his people, the sheep of his pasture," says the Psalmist King David. (Psalm 100:3, NIV)

(b) Therefore, King David says about God in Psalm 23: "The Lord is my [our] shepherd... (Psalm 23:1, NIV). And then he continues to show in the remaining verses of Psalm 23, how God shepherds us by being "a loving Father": He is our provider, savior, protector, guide, deliverer, comforter, soul restorer, and source of peace, goodness, mercy, and shelter.

5. TO BE A SAFE REFUGE AND FORTRESS FOR US:

(a) "The eternal God is our refuge, and underneath are the everlasting arms," says Deuteronomy 33:27, in the NIV Bible.

(b) "God is our refuge and strength, an ever present help in trouble," says Psalm 46:1, in the NIV.

(c) "He who dwells in the shelter of the Most High will rest under the shadow of the almighty. I will say of the

Lord, 'He is my refuge and my fortress'...." (Psalm 91:1, NIV).

6. GOOD HEALTH:

(a) "Praise the Lord, O my soul, and forget not all his benefits—who forgives all your sins and heals all your diseases, who redeems your life from the pit and crowns you with love and compassion," says King David, in Psalm 103:2-3, in the NIV Bible.

(b) God sent Jesus Christ on earth, so that "He himself [Jesus], bore our sins [and sicknesses] in his body on the tree [of Calvary's wooden cross], so that we might die to sin and live for righteousness [a holy and healthy life]; by his wounds you have been healed" (1 Peter 2:24, NIV).

(c) So, "Many are the afflictions of the righteous [and redeemed], but the Lord preserves him from them all... The Lord preserves him completely" (Psalm 34:19-20, NKJV Bible).

(d) "If you listen to the voice of the Lord your God and do what is right in his eyes... I [the Lord] will not bring on you any of the diseases I brought on the Egyptians, for I am the Lord who heals thee" (Exodus 15:26, NIV).

(e) "The Lord will keep you free from every disease" (Deuteronomy 7:15, NIV).

7. REDEMPTION FROM SIN FOR ALL THOSE WHO REPENT AND BELIEVE IN CHRIST JESUS:

(a) "For God so loved the world [all sinful humanity] that he gave his one and only Son, that whoever believes in him shall not perish but have eternal life. For God did not send his Son into the world to condemn the world, but to save the world through him" (John 3:16-17, NIV).

(b) "Therefore, there is now no condemnation for those who are in Christ Jesus, because through Christ Jesus the law of the Spirit of life set me [and you also] free from the law of sin and death. For what the [Mosaic] law was powerless to do in that it was weakened by the sinful nature, God did by sending his own Son in the likeness of sinful man, in order that the righteous requirements of the law [given to Moses] might be fully met in us, who do not live [constantly] according to the sinful nature but according to the Spirit." (Romans 8:1-4, NIV)

(c) "...God demonstrates his own love for us in this: While we were still sinners, Christ died for us." (Romans 5:8, NIV)

(d) "Consequently, just as the result of one trespass [Adam and Eve's sin] was condemnation for all men, so also the result of one act of righteousness [Jesus' death on Calvary's cross] was justification that brings life [freedom] for all men." (Romans 5:18, NIV)

(e) "It is for freedom that Christ has set us free." (Galatians 5:1, NIV)

(f) "....We have been 'justified' [or exonerated by God] through faith [in Jesus Christ]; we have peace with God through our Lord Jesus Christ, through whom we have gained access by faith into the grace in which we now stand."(Romans 5:1, NIV)

(g) "For he [God] has rescued us from the dominion of darkness and brought us into the kingdom of the Son he loves, in whom we have redemption, the forgiveness of sins." (Colossians 1:13, NIV)

8. DELIVERANCE FROM PRIDE:

"The sacrifices of God are a broken spirit; a broken and contrite heart" (Psalm 51:17, NIV).

For God to use you and me He must first get rid of all our pride: He must break us down by emptying us of all our self-worship (or pride), like Satan. We have to be big enough to become small enough for Him to use us; so that we will be humble and contrite enough for and in ministry service. Humility and a contrite heart make a believer fit for different kinds of kingdom ministry. But sincere humility at its best with God's special anointing, qualifies a believer for exaltation and designated responsibility with power, for special Kingdom ministry. Consequently, God knows that the deadliest sin that can stand between man and Himself for special kingdom service is man's pride; and that was what confused Satan and caused him to say to God, "I will not serve." Like Satan, some men get so proud of their negative plans and its success, or good achievements in this world, that they have an attitude that suggests that they will not humbly serve the Creator [God], but rather, the creature [Satan]. And indeed, some of them do serve the creature Satan! It's only a matter of time before they come up against an impenetrable brick-wall situation, (like an incurable or terminal disease like cancer, for example), which usually forces them to humbly go down on their knees to beg for Almighty

God's help for healing, and admit through their sufferings and subsequent divine healing, that "God is sovereign": He is the Greatest Physician; Creator and Sustainer of the universe and all beings; Ruler of our lives; and that His mighty healing power through the Great Physician (Christ Jesus), is inexplicably awesome. And all men can and will come to know that divine miraculous healing could only be experienced by a believer or unbeliever, only when and after his selfish pride and arrogance has been emptied out or subdued. Then, his humble testimony of God's healing action in his life can be personally, privately, and publicly declared and acknowledged, and that God's loving-kindness and His grace and mercy for all men will be specially known and seen, by all those who are lost in trespasses, (including all unbelievers and backsliders). Consequently also, so that all the redeemed and the righteous human souls on fire for God will be encouraged, and grow stronger in faith, courage, strength, and confidence, whilst they labor in God's vineyard.

9. WISDOM:

"If any of you lacks wisdom, he should ask God, who gives generously to all without finding fault, and it will be given him," says James 1:5, in the NIV Bible.

10. TO LEAD US ALONG THE RIGHT PATH:

(a) "He guides me in paths of righteousness for his name's sake" (Psalm 23:3, NIV).

(b) "Your word is a lamp to my feet and a light for my path" (Psalm 119:105, NIV).

(c) "Good and upright is the Lord; therefore he instructs sinners in the way. He guides the humble in what is right and teaches them his way" (Psalm 25:8-9, NIV).

11. DELIVERANCE IN TIMES OF TRIAL AND TEMPTATION:

(a) "Dear friends, do not be surprised at the painful trial you are suffering, as though something strange were happening to you. But rejoice that you participate in the sufferings of Christ, so that you may be overjoyed when his glory is revealed" (1 Peter 4:12-13, NIV).

(b) "No temptation has seized you except what is common to man. And God is faithful; he will not let you be tempted beyond what you can bear. But when you are tempted, he will also provide a way out so that you can stand up under it" (1 Corinthians 10:13, NIV).

12. DELIVERANCE FROM ALL OUR FEARS:

(a) "Fear Him ye saints and you will have nothing else to fear; make you His service your delight, your wants [including your deliverance from fear] shall be His cares" (Taken from the Anglican hymn book, "Ancient and Modern").

(b) "I sought the Lord and he answered me; he delivered me from all my fears" (Psalm 34:4, NIV).

(c) "The Lord is my light and my salvation—whom shall I fear? The Lord is the stronghold of my life—of whom shall I be afraid? When evil men advance against me to devour my flesh, when my enemies and my foes attack me, they will stumble and fall. Though an army besiege me my heart will not fear; though war break out against me, even then will I be confident" (Psalm 27:1-3, NIV).

(d) So, "Be strong and courageous. Do not be terrified; do not be discouraged, for the Lord your God will be with you wherever you go" (Joshua 1:9, NIV).

(e) "For he did not give you a spirit of timidity [fear], but a spirit of power, of love and self-confidence [self-control, or a sound mind, as the NKJV puts it]" (2 Timothy 1:7, NIV).

13.GIVES US PEACE, FAITH, GRACE, HOPE, AND LOVE:

(a) St. Paul says in Romans 5:1-5, NIV, "Therefore, since we have been justified through faith, we have 'peace' with God through our Lord Jesus Christ, through whom we have gained access by 'faith' into this 'grace' in which we now stand. And we rejoice in the 'hope' of the glory of God... And hope does not disappoint us, because God has poured out his 'love' into our hearts by the Holy Spirit, whom he has given us."

14. HAPPINESS, PROSPERITY, AND LONGEVITY, WHEN WE LIVE RIGHTEOUSLY (OR IN THE FEAR OF THE LORD):

> (a) "Come, my children, [says King David], listen to me; I will teach you the fear of the Lord.
> Whoever of you loves life and desires to see many good days [happiness, peace, joy, health, and longevity], keep your tongue from evil and your lips from speaking lies [which also includes gossip and slander]. Turn from evil and do good; seek peace and pursue it... The face of the Lord is against those who do evil... A righteous man

may have many troubles, but the Lord delivers him from them all" (Psalm 34:11-19, NIV).

(b) And in Psalm 128:1-6, the Psalmist gives further counsel: "Blessed are all who fear the Lord, who walk in his ways [righteousness]. You will eat the fruit of your labor; blessings and prosperity will be yours. Your wife will be like a fruitful vine within your house; your sons will be like olive shoots around your table. Thus is the man blessed who fears the Lord...and may you live to see your children's children."

(c) Again he assures us, "Blessed [or happy] is the man who does not walk in the counsel of the wicked or stand in the way of sinners or sit in the seat of mockers. But his delight is in the law of the Lord, and on his law he meditates day and night... Whatever he does prospers" (Psalm 1:1-3, NIV).

(d) And, "With long life I will satisfy him and show him my salvation" (Psalm 91:16, NIV).

15. HE RESTORES OUR SOUL:

(a) "....He restores my soul" (Psalm 23:3, NIV).

16. HE GIVES US SPIRITUAL JOY, HOPE, AND PEACE, AS RENEWED STRENGTH TO CONQUER GRIEF:

(b) "Do not grieve, for the joy of the Lord is your strength" (Nehemiah 8:10, NIV)

(c) "Those who hope in the Lord will renew their strength" (Isaiah 40:31, NIV).

(d) 'Great peace have they who love the Law, and nothing can make them stumble" (Psalm 119:165, NIV).

17. HE PROMISES US REVELATION KNOWLEDGE ABOUT HIMSELF, THROUGH CHRIST JESUS:

(a) "I and the Father are one," says Jesus, in John 10:10, NIV.

(b) "Who has seen me has seen the Father," Jesus also says in John 14:9, NIV. Jesus was referring to His immortal image like the Father, just like the immortal image of the created Adam, before he sinned in the Garden of Eden. Sin made Adam mortal.

(c) Still speaking in John 6:44, NIV about God, Jesus says about our salvation, "No one can come to me unless the Father who sent me draws him."

(d) Again Jesus said about His Father, "The Father loves the Son and has placed everything in his hands" (John 3:35, NIV). So Jesus has unlimited power to judge all creation on Judgment Day!

(e) And since God is spirit, and those who worship Him must do so in spirit and in truth, Jesus says in John 6:46, NIV, "No one has seen the Father [which means, only Him]." What we have seen and experienced of God through Him, is all that we know spiritually about God; since He (Jesus) is also one of the three Persons of the Blessed Trinity. Therefore, Jesus says in Matthew 11:27, "No one knows the Father except the Son." Because Jesus is God's Son and He came down to earth from heaven (God's domain).

Section 17(e) above only proves to us that God is so very awesome, because we cannot behold Him completely, or His total presence; for He has a mysterious and infinite spirit presence, with no beginning or end. So our finite mind cannot contain, fathom, explain, or understand Him or His ways.

Over the years and even in biblical times, we know and can speak of or about Him in His physical and spiritual manifestations and revelations in Jesus Christ's likeness on earth, and as a cloud, a fire, and like a burning bush, in the Old Testament biblical times, for example.

We also see God's likeness of character in and through Christ Jesus, as a very compassionate and loving father, who is an awesome and powerful being; for even the wind and waves (or sea) obey Him. He shows mercy and forgiveness in all His ways, but as a just judge and a jealous protector of His people (Israel) and all those who fear Him. You can't serve Him and Satan together. He is also a generous provider of our physical and spiritual needs, a healer of all diseases, a counsellor, a wise teacher, a comforter, a friend, a guide, and a source of pure wisdom and understanding. God is so awesome and powerful, that Moses could not fearlessly behold Him or even stand in His presence on Mount Sinai without removing his sandals (Exodus 3:5). Afterwards, when Moses went back to report to his people about his encounter with Almighty God, his people (Israel) thought that he had seen a Ghost—just because his face was so transformed and radiant through and by "God's Shakina glory."*

18. PROMISES US NEW LIFE THROUGH CHRIST JESUS:

(a) John 3:16 says, "For God so loved the world that he gave his one and only Son, that whoever believes in him shall not perish but have eternal life." And in John 10:10, NIV, Jesus says, "I am come that they may have life and have it to the full." Jesus is referring to God's package of "salvation" and "eternal life," together.

(b) "Therefore, if anyone is in Christ, he is a new creation [a new or changed person]; the old has gone, the new [person] has come. All this is from God, who reconciled us to himself through Christ..." [God is referring to a radical transformation and renewal of body, soul, mind and spirit, or regeneration through Christ Jesus (2 Corinthians 5:17, NIV)].

(c) And, "I tell you the truth, no one can enter the kingdom of God unless he is born of water [water baptism] and the Spirit [Holy Spirit baptism]," says Jesus, in John 3:5, NIV.

(d) Again says Jesus, in Matthew 18:2, NIV, "I tell you the truth, unless you change [in character and disposition] and become like little children, [or be humble and have simple faith, wonder, and obedience], you will never enter the kingdom of heaven."

(e) If you do change, or become born-again, "Then you will know the truth [Jesus], and the truth will set you free" (John 8:32, NIV).

(f) You must "Seek first his kingdom and his righteousness, and all these things [spiritual, material, physical, intellectual, and emotional blessings] will be given to you as well" (Matthew 6:33, NIV).

(g) You must also confess your sins and forsake them. And, since God is faithful and just, He will forgive your sins and cleanse you of all unrighteousness. (1 John 1:9)

(h) "Those who hope in the Lord shall renew their strength" (Isaiah 40:30, NIV).

(i) "And we know that in all things God works for the good of those who love him, who have been called according to his purpose" (Romans 8:28, NIV).

19. GRACE, MERCY, AND PEACE, FOR A NEW LIFE OF "DIVINE ORDER" TO PREVAIL DURING TRYING TIMES:

In this new life of grace, mercy, and peace, called "life to the full" or "abundant life through Christ Jesus," the redeemed and the righteous human souls on fire for God have a tremendous amount of favor, power, responsibility, and authority through Christ Jesus; because they have now become "new creations" (2 Corinthians 5:17): meaning that they are now responsible for practicing and maintaining a life of righteousness through Christ Jesus, whilst God also has to play His part by helping them to maintain this "new life." God has to be a God of power, authority, grace, mercy, and justice, for "Divine Order"* to prevail continually on their behalf, when expressing His loving-kindness and favor for them. He has to protect, heal, console, counsel, guide, forgive, provide food, shelter and clothing for them, and be their safe refuge in times of trouble, as well as lead them along paths of righteousness. So that when or if He punishes them or withholds something good from them, for example, as a just father and righteous judge, this does not mean that He does not love them. For His justice could or may be either reward, compassion, or punishment, depending on the situation; but it is always with the intention of drawing them closer to Him in love, reverence, humility, patience, wisdom, and self-control, to foster peace, love, stability and harmony (or Divine Order) in this world.

God hates sin but loves the sinner. So this is where His grace, mercy, peace and justice comes into the picture for the redeemed and the righteous. He loves the redeemed and the righteous so specially, because they are not practicing (or habitual) sinners like the unrighteous, and they fear Him. Therefore, His grace, mercy, and justice dished out to them through their faith in Christ Jesus, are always given to them as an unmerited favor. So the redeemed and righteous qualify for God's mercy and compassion, in this way; and this privilege in itself is great favor, and continues with authority and power over the unrighteous. But still, we are all sinners! Had it not been for God's grace (or undeserved favor) and His loving-kindness or mercy, through Christ Jesus, all of us (including the redeemed and righteous) would already have been condemned and consumed, or hell-bound.

When we repent of our sins or sin and become "new creations," or born-again believers, we become adopted by God as His sons and daughters, because we no longer have fellowship with Satan, and God's grace, mercy, loving-kindness, peace, and justice, control our lives.

1 Peter 2:9 says, that we have become, "A royal priesthood, a holy nation, a chosen people, a people belonging to God, that you [or we] may declare the praises of him who called you [or us] out of darkness into his wonderful light."

God's grace, mercy, justice, peace, and loving-kindness, control the lives of the redeemed and the righteous, only because of the indwelling power of Christ Jesus and the Holy Spirit.

Consequently, His grace, peace, and mercy, is always sufficient for us believers, and He does not always punish us as we deserve, for our iniquities (Psalm 103:10); nor does He harbor His anger against us forever (Psalm 103:9). So Psalm 107:1 says, in the NKJV Bible, "Give thanks unto the Lord for he is good, for his mercy endureth forever."

Now since God has a special love for the redeemed and the righteous, He demonstrates His love and justice for them by punishing all those who "mess with them," or use and abuse them. And He gives them the power of prayer and sufficient grace, mercy, and patience, to endure and overcome hard testing. Psalm 34:19-22, KJV, confirms this truth, as the Psalmist addresses it as follows:

> "Many are the afflictions of the righteous [and the redeemed]: but the Lord delivereth him out of them all. He keepeth all his bones: not one of them is broken. Evil shall slay the wicked: and they that hate the righteous shall be desolate. The Lord redeemeth the soul of his servants: and none of them that trust in him shall be desolate."

The letter of James, chapter 5 verse 16, also says, "The effectual fervent prayer of the righteous man availeth much"—or has a powerful effect, as the GNB puts it.

So the fervent prayers of the redeemed and the righteous on their knees, with a strong faith in Almighty God through faith in the power of Christ Jesus and the Holy Spirit, is the most formidable weapon of the righteous and redeemed believer on earth. Any other reciprocal means to achieve their ends or resolve other human conflict and problems, only breeds violence and more violence; and finally, chaos, disaster, and destruction results. Therefore, the prophet Zachariah says, in Zachariah 4:6, in the NIV Bible, "Not by might, nor by power, but by my spirit says the Lord Almighty."

"For the Lord is a God of justice," says Isaiah 30:18, in the NIV. "Power and might are in your [His] hand, and no one can withstand you [Him]," says 2 Chronicles 20:6, in the NIV Bible.

Therefore, God's powerful biblical promises with His positive, awesome assurances for the redeemed and the righteous—through His mercy, grace, wisdom, truth, loving-kindness, peace, protection, and other provisions, establishes "Divine Order"* and justice in the world, and in the life of every believer in Christ Jesus. For God is mysteriously and incredibly omnipotent, omniscient, omnipresent, holy, loving, compassionate, and just, and His assured promises with their positive rewards are unlimited and very valuable, for our salvation and eternal life.

"Let us praise and bless His holy name!"

7

THE REDEEMED AND THE RIGHTEOUS' JOYFUL, EARTHLY-SPIRITUAL-STRUGGLES, TO SECURE AND MAINTAIN "GOD'S ABUNDANT-LIFE PACKAGE"

On page 15 of "A Gardener's Little Devotional Book," Philip Yancey has been quoted as saying, "Some of us seem so anxious about avoiding hell that we forget to celebrate our journey [on earth] towards heaven."

And how do we do that? Joyfully in the Lord of course! Let me explain to you what it entails.

When you were redeemed and then afterwards became "a born-again believer," or "a new creation" (as 2 Corinthians 5:17 says), and were given "new life" (or regenerated through Christ Jesus), you became "a promisee"* of "God's abundant-life package," through Christ Jesus (John 10:10). Consequently, there was and are still some important issues that you had and must still seriously observe, consider, and obey, during your earthly, spiritual journey. Namely:

(a) Love God with all your heart, with all your soul, with your mind, and with all your strength; and, love your neighbor as your-self. All the Mosaic Law and the Prophets hang on and cling to these two Commandments of Jesus (Matthew 22:37-40).

(b) Then, if you are humble enough and obedient to God by keep-ing these two above Commandments, you will live victoriously; for the Lord will subdue your pride and guide you continually. As Psalm 25 verse 3, 9-10, and verse 14, in the GNB says, "Defeat does not come to those who trust in you [God], but to those who are quick to rebel against you... [For] He [God] leads the humble in the right way and teaches them his will. With faithfulness and love he leads all who keep his covenant and obey his commands... The Lord is the friend of those who obey him and he affirms his covenant with them." (For He is a covenant keeping God).

(c) You must also cast all your burdens and anxieties on Jesus, be-cause He compassionately cares for and about you (1 Peter 5:7); and He can solve all your problems.

(d) Let the Joy of the Lord be your strength (Nehemiah 8:10), and delight yourself in Him (Psalm 37:4). For without Him you are nothing and can do nothing.

(e) Finally, celebrate your abundant life anointing joyfully, through faith in Christ Jesus—after your newly-found gifts of the fruit of the Holy Spirit, of love, joy, peace, patience, self-control, humility, kindness, faithfulness, and gentleness (Galatians 5:22-23), and your faith and hope in God's love, grace, justice, peace and mercy, through Christ Jesus.

Now, "If you can forgive the person you were, [before you were saved], accept the person you are, [now], and believe in the person you will become, [through faith in Christ Jesus], you are headed for joy [complete earthly and heavenly joy]. So celebrate your life [now]."

The above quote was taken from page 15 of "A Gardener's Little Devotional Book," by Barbara Johnson. As a new believer feeding on the milk of Holy Scripture, I will continue to make my writing very comprehensive for you to digest.

Notwithstanding, hear what one wise man (Leonard Ravenhill) had to say on page 41 of "A Gardener's Little Devotional Book"—about when making decisions and following through with them when celebrating your abundant life's joyful, earthly spiritual-struggles: "Men give advice, God gives guidance."

And Proverbs 20:24 says, "A man's steps are directed by the Lord. How then can anyone understand his own way?"

Therefore, even though a man has many plans in his mind and heart to execute, and he may have many advisors (carnal or spiritual), it is the Lord's purpose that will prevail. For God is always in control. "Whatever He does not allow, He prevents; and whatever He allows He does not prevent," say the old people in my country. And not even Satan can alter God's plans or Judgements for you and me—although we have a free-will to make our own choices. So, all Bible prophecy for our life or world events must be fulfilled or come to pass as written, and according to God's timing and will.

Hence, it is always better for all the redeemed and righteous human souls on fire to take advice from and obey God's wise counsel for their lives, from the Holy Bible. And sometimes, they should also take refuge in the wise counsel of God's experienced anointed holy persons, after testing their spirit—because no one is perfect. But most times, you can't go wrong when you seek wise counsel from the lord and His righteous people, about every decision that you have to make. For this is also how many wise persons prosper: they shun the advice and ways of evil men, so that they can also become more Christ-like and Holy Spirit filled to do God's will.

Consequently, this is what a wise man like King Solomon has to say in Proverbs 3:5-10, to all God's righteous and redeemed people, whilst they are joyfully struggling on earth and celebrating "their abundant life through Christ Jesus," before they go to their eternal home in glory:

> "Trust in the Lord with all your heart and lean not on your own understanding; in all your ways acknowledge him and he will make your path straight. Do not be wise in your own eyes; fear the Lord and shun evil. This will bring health to your body and nourishment to your bones... Honor the Lord with your wealth, with the first fruits of all your crops; then your barn will be filled to overflowing, and your vats will brim over with new wine."

This is very sound advice and guidance indeed from King Solomon. What King Solomon previously stated in Proverbs 3:5-10, was also seriously emphasized in Psalm 128 by his father (King David), about how a righteous or redeemed person can secure and maintain good values and the advantages of an "abundant life," (or prosperity), through a healthy, holy, and blessed life that pleases God, during his joyful earthly struggles. It's not only for and in material, spiritual, and financial issues that this holds true, but also for and in family-life relationships as well. It's all about "righteous living," through "the fear if the Lord."

In Psalm 128, King David attests to and verifies this fact:

> "Blessed [or happy] are all those who fear the Lord, who walk in his ways. You will eat the fruit of your labor; bless-ing and prosperity will be yours. Your wife will be like a fruitful vine within your house; your sons will be like olive

shoots around your table. Thus is the man blessed who fears the Lord. May the Lord bless you from Zion all the days of your life; may you see the prosperity of Jerusalem [or your homeland], and may you live to see your children's children."

This is a situation on earth which calls not only for our celebration for God's provision of all our material needs, but also for generating and maintaining peace, love, unity, and happiness in our home, and all our family-life relationships—especially longevity to see our children's children, and enjoying peace on our borders with our neighbors. Sirach 25, in the GNB, (as in Ecclesiasticus 25 in the Old King James Version Bible), says, "Three things the Lord loves to see": a husband and wife who are well matched or live in peace; neighbors that live in peace with each other; and brothers and sisters who live together in peace and unity: this is God's heritage for all His redeemed and righteous people.

So despite how many trials, temptations, afflictions, and persecutions that beset and besiege the redeemed and righteous human souls, whilst on fire for God during their earthly struggles, they will always be happy and celebrate God's abundant-life gifts—because "The joy of the Lord is my [their] strength" (Nehemiah 8:10), and they delight themselves in Him (Psalm 37:4). He is also their light and their salvation, says Psalm 27:1; their protector and refuge in times of trouble (Psalm 91); and has promised to supply all their needs (Philippians 4:19), as long as they delight themselves in Him (Psalm 37:4). And, with all the temptations and trials that besiege the redeemed and righteous, God always makes a way out for them where and when there seem to be no way.

Jesus Christ and the Holy Spirit also helps the redeemed and the righteous to overcome and forget all memories of their past fears, failures, disappointments, bad habits, and evil desires, and to put on the full armor of God (Ephesians 6:11-18), so that they can have Jesus Christ and Holy Spirit's power and faith, to pray fervently to protect themselves against all spiritual attacks and wickedness in high places, and have the peace of Christ within them at all times, to wage warfare against Satan and his cohorts, and to pull down their strongholds.

With this "new life in Christ Jesus," God expects all believers to live righteously, so that Satan will not steal their joyful blessings of "abundant life." God has therefore put in place many "righteous demands," through "the fruit of the Holy Spirit" and "Jesus Christ's teachings," that we have to obey. And as long as we live on this earth, these righteous demands for acquisition of God's promised blessings will haunt us, if we become disobedient.

Let me now list some of God's righteous covenant demands which He expects us to obey, during our joyful earthly struggles to secure and maintain our abundant life:

1. Take care of the poor and the destitute (Matthew 25:31-36);

2. Take care of the widows and orphans who are in distress (James 1:27);

3. "Be joyful always, pray continually; give thanks in all circumstances; for this is God's will for you in Christ Jesus" (1 Thessalonians 5:16, NIV);

4. Read God's Holy Word day and night (Psalm 1:1-2);

5. "Love your neighbor as yourself" (Matthew 22:39, NIV);

6. "Love your enemies, bless those who curse you, do good to them that hate you, and pray for them who persecute you" (Matthew 5:44, NIV);

7. "Seek peace and pursue it" (Psalm 34:13, NIV); "Be a peace maker" (Matthew 5:9, NIV);

8. "Keep your tongue from evil and your lips from speaking lies" (Psalm 34:13, NIV);

9. Have a spirit of forgiveness (Matthew 6:14; Ephesians 4:32, NIV);

10. Encourage each other, especially in righteousness (1 Thessalonians 5:11);

11. "Share with God's people who are in need. Practice hospitality" (Romans 12:13);

12. "Have faith in God" (Mark 11:22, NIV);

13. Conquer worry, doubt, fear and anxiety, through faith in God (Matthew 6: 25-34, NIV);

14. Conquer pride and selfishness (Philippians 2:3-4, NIV);

15. Have a humble and contrite heart (Psalm 51:17, NIV);

16. Help one another with each other's burdens (Galatians 6:2, NIV);

17. "I am sending you out [into the world] just like sheep to a pack of wolves. You must be as cautious as snakes and as gentle as doves" (Matthew 10:16, GNB);

18. Accept and believe God's promises; for "God is not a man that he should lie" (Numbers 23:19, NIV);

19. Be "the salt of the earth" (Matthew 5:13);

20. Be "the light of the world" (Matthew 5:14);

21. Take up your cross daily and follow Jesus—not physically like He did, but symbolically, sacrificially, and selflessly in our life's struggles, with the same spirit of commitment, perseverance, and humility, which He demonstrated on His way to Calvary: meaning that, no matter how heavy and overwhelming the cross (or problem) may seem, don't run away from it; try to carry it or solve the problem. If you can't carry it, remember that God never gives His righteous and redeemed people more burdens than they can bear; He will always send an angel or a good person, (a good Samaritan), to help you. All you have to do is just call upon "the name of Jesus," with faith and hope, and your problem will be solved—just like when the cross overwhelmed Jesus on His way to Calvary, and God sent Simon of Cyrene, a Good Samaritan, to help Him. So fear not! Ask for Jesus' help joyfully, for Jesus is always only a prayer away and He is able to help you;

22. "Worship the Lord in the beauty of holiness" (Psalm 96:9, NIV);

23. Praise and bless Him joyfully and continually, as King David did (Psalm 34:1);

24. Keep the law of the Lord in your heart: the Ten Commandments, in Deuteronomy 5:6-21. Guard it well, and try your best to obey it. Be a doer and not just a hearer of God's Holy Word (James 1:22). September 7th. 1999 issue of "Our Daily Bread" puts it even better: "Let God's Word, [His righteous covenant demands with us] fill your mind, rule your heart, and guide your tongue."

25. Finally, for you to be able to keep God's righteous covenant demands, you must be "born-again" or spiritually transformed, (or regenerated), and you will see the kingdom of heaven (John 3:3)—yes, only see it! And better works of righteousness will begin to follow or proceed from you. But, what is most important or essential for you is, you must be born of water (or receive water baptism), and the baptism of the Holy Spirit, to become "a new creation"; so that you can enter the kingdom of heaven (John 3:5). Yes, for to enter the Kingdom of heaven is more important than to only just see or view it from afar.

These are the most important steps a believer "must take," before he can be fully accepted into the body of believers in Christ Jesus, to become "a saint," (or citizen of heaven). And at this point in time in a new believer's life, his or her joyful, earthly, spiritual-struggles against Satan's temptations and God's trials (or testing), will begin "in full force."

Alexander Maclaren says to a born-again believer, that temptation will say to him, "Do this pleasant thing: do not be hindered by the fact that it is wrong."

And trials (or testing) will say, "Do the right and noble thing; do not be hindered by the fact that it is painful."

Surely, Satan is the author of our temptations, and God is the author of our trials.

God sends us trials and allows Satan to tempt us daily, so that we will grow stronger in faith and hope, each time we overcome them, by activating our faith, patience, perseverance, and hope, successfully; so that one day, we will be in line to receive our heavenly crown.

Whilst Satan appeals to our weakest and strongest emotions and desires to bring out the worst in us, God tests us to bring out the best in us.

Therefore, James 1:2, in the NIV Bible, says, "Consider it pure joy my brothers, whenever you face trials [or tests] of many kinds, because you know that by testing your faith develops perseverance. Perseverance must finish its work so that you may be mature and complete, not lacking anything."

And so, St. Paul says, "Be joyful in hope, patient in affliction, faithful in prayer" (Romans 12:12, NIV).

Prayer must never be left out of the equation in our joyful, earthly-struggles; for many more problems have been solved through the fervent prayers of the redeemed and righteous, than by human might and power.

So, as we joyfully try our best to observe and keep God's righteous covenant demands, with the help of His grace and mercy, our prayers, the wise counsel and guidance of the Holy Spirit, and the peace of Christ Jesus, God safely guides us continually. And He will never leave us comfortless or forsake us.

In Psalm 16, verse 11, King David said to Him, "Thou wilt shew me the path of life: in thy presence is fullness of joy; and at thy right hand are pleasures for evermore."

We can quote the same phrase to God for ourselves, like King David, since Jesus Christ has resurrected and ascended to heaven, and is now sitting at the right hand of God interceding on our behalf—especially when we are tempted to sin and/or fall short of God's righteous covenant demands on earth.

As our "High Priest"* and "advocate"* in heaven, Jesus Christ has already made it possible for us to go boldly and straight to God's throne of grace with our petitions, and find grace and mercy. The unrighteous do not have this privilege. Therefore, we (the redeemed and the righteous) have absolute victory and power through Christ Jesus, because we are no longer lost in trespasses or condemned sinners like the unrighteous. Jesus has already paid the price for our sins and also given us an eternal assurance of joy and hope that one day, heaven will be our eternal home.

So, as we suffer and struggle with trials and temptations on this earth, as Christians, we are doing so with spiritual joy and hope, as we look forward to and for our complete eternal freedom from all our earthly sinful shackles, to receive our eternal heavenly rewards: the rewards that we earn through our obedience to God's righteous covenant-demands, because God always keeps His promise.

1 Peter 4:12-20, in the GNB, says to us about our trials,

> "My dear friends, do not be surprised at the painful test you are suffering, as though something unusual were happening to you. Rather be glad that you are sharing in Christ's suffering, so that you may be full of joy when his glory is revealed. Happy are you if you are insulted because you are Christ's followers; this means that the glorious Spirit, the Spirit of God, is resting on you. If any of you suffers, it must not be because he is a murderer or a thief or a criminal or meddles in other people's affairs. However, if you suffer because you are a Christian, don't be ashamed of it, but thank God that you bear Christ's name...So then, those who suffer because it is God's will for them, should by their good actions trust themselves completely to their Creator, who always keeps his promise."

And in 1 Corinthians 10:13, in the NIV Bible, St. Paul says about temptation, "No temptation has seized you except what is common to man. And God is faithful; he will not let you be tempted beyond what you can bear. But when you are tempted, he will also provide a way out so that you can stand up under it." And yet, even though you are a redeemed, born-again, baptized-believer, and God has promised you deliverance from your trials and temptations, you will still or occasionally find yourself doing the evil things that you do not want to do. This is because of the influence and resurfacing of your "old self," or sinful Adamic-nature, which you have not completely conquered or got rid of.

Thanks to God for sending us His Son (Jesus Christ), to deliver us from this Adamic or old criminal nature. Jesus shed His precious blood on Calvary's wooden cross for us, so that we would be redeemed (or exonerated and cleansed) from this curse and its deserved punishment in and on our life. Through Christ Jesus, God cleansed us whiter than snow and forgave us of all our unrighteousness (or our past sins).

Let me now say that being righteous or cleansed from all your past unrighteousness as a new believer, does not mean that in future you will still remain free from sin. It just means that you will sin occasionally, but no longer be "a practicing sinner"* like your "old self." And that you have decided to trust and obey God, through your faith in Jesus Christ and His righteousness, to keep you safe and secured in times of trials and temptation, through God's love, grace, and mercy. For, had it not been for God's love, grace, and mercy, and our faith in Christ Jesus, we would already have been condemned and consumed for our sins.

Hebrews 12:28 says, ".... Let us be thankful, and so worship God acceptably with reverence and awe, for our God is a consuming fire."

Therefore, our obedience option to God's righteous covenant demands is based on both of our choices, (favorable or unfavorable response), to His love, grace, and mercy, which are of paramount importance for the salvation of the redeemed and the righteous believers on earth.

By trusting God and trying your best to obey Him, in faith, humility, faithfulness, patience, wisdom, righteousness, and perseverance, the redeemed and the righteous person becomes more self-confident, courageous, more faithful, Holy Spirit-filled, supernaturally powerful, more joyful, more peaceful, wiser, more compassionate and loving, more joyful, more self-controlled, patient, and full of hope. And he finally begins to realize and say like St. Paul:

>"If God is for us, who can be against us? He who did not spare his own Son, but gave him up for us all—how will he not also, along with him [Jesus] graciously give us all things [all the rewards for obeying His righteous covenant demands]? Who will bring any charges against whom God has chosen? It is God who justifies. Who is he that condemns? Christ Jesus [the righteous judge], who died—more than that, who was raised to life—is at the right hand of God and is also interceding for us" (Romans 8:31-34, NIV).

>[So] "Therefore, there is now no condemnation for those who are in Christ Jesus, because through Christ Jesus the law of the Spirit of life [of God's love, grace, and mercy] set me free from the law of sin and death" (Romans 8:1, NIV).

>"In all things we are more than conquerors through him [both God and Jesus] who loved us" (Romans 8:37, NIV).

>"And we know that in all things God works for the good of those who love him, who have been called according to his purpose" (Romans 8:28, NIV).

St. Paul therefore concludes about our present joyful, spiritual struggles and sufferings on this earth—before Jesus Christ's final coming to judge all creation and to reward us for our obedience to God's righteous covenant demands: "I consider that our present sufferings are not worth comparing with the glory that will be revealed in us ...." (Romans 8:18, NIV).

Therefore, during the redeemed and the righteous' joyful, earthly struggles and sufferings from their trials and temptations, they must show their continual obedience and gratefulness to God, Jesus, and the Holy Spirit, through their ceaseless praise, blessings, worship, and thanksgiving, for helping them to secure and maintain "Christ's abundant life package," mentioned in John 10:10, before going to receive their blissful heavenly reward of eternal life and glory.

They must also always remember to specially celebrate the work of Our Savior (Jesus Christ), who died in our place to save us from sin, death, and hell, on Calvary's wooden cross; so that Satan and the gates of hell could not prevail against God's church on earth. And most of all, believers should be mindful to celebrate "the joy of the Lord" at all times, for it is not only their strength, but also their consolation-weapon for maintaining a positive, joyful, and satisfied mind and heart condition through Christ Jesus, which helps us to nullify Satan's vicious schemes and occasional attacks of despair, depression, discouragement, faithlessness, and hopelessness, about God's assured eternal heavenly promises and rewards for us.

Finally, one of Satan's most formidable weapons of discouragement and destruction to annihilate the redeemed and the righteous human souls on fire for God, as they joyfully struggle and celebrate their journey towards heaven, (on earth), is the loose talk of unbelievers and some believers. Proverbs 10:19, in the NIV Bible, say, "He who holds his tongue is wise, [especially an evil tongue]." For, "Death and life are in the power of the tongue," says Proverbs 18:21, in the NKJV. It is alleged that the evil and loose tongue of men has destroyed more positive minds and innocent people in good human relationships, (like in many faithful marriages and good friendships), and has put to death more people in this world than all the world wars put together. Therefore, James 3:8 says, "No one has been able to tame the tongue!" The same tongue that we use to praise God is the same tongue that we use to curse or destroy our fellow-man. Character assassination is a common thing. This means that more people in this world are guilty of, or at some time, have maliciously spoken or uttered a careless word about another person, in their life time. If you have not done that, count yourself specially blessed by Almighty God.

Therefore, Jesus said in Matthew 5:11-12, in the NIV—to encourage and console all the redeemed and the righteous human souls on fire for God: "Blessed are you when people insult you, persecute you and falsely say all kinds of evil against you because of me. Rejoice and be glad, because great is your reward in heaven, for in the same way they persecuted the prophets before you."

So let me finally add my two cents bit of encouragement for all the redeemed and the righteous people, in their joyful, earthly, spiritual-struggles.

Do not be weary of doing good, and do not be discouraged or forsaken about your eternal heavenly hope; for you will surely and finally overcome Satan and his disciples in this world. Jesus Christ said in John 16:33, NIV, "In this world you will have trouble, but I have overcome the world." So you too can do likewise, implied Christ Jesus. Consequently, St. Paul said in 1 Corinthians 1:8-9, that "He [Jesus] will keep you strong to the end, so that you will be blameless on the day of the Lord Jesus Christ [Judgment Day]. [For] God, who has called you into fellowship with his Son Jesus Christ our Lord, is faithful."

So God's earthly righteous covenant demands are not too difficult or impossible for you to keep. You must walk and talk with the Lord Jesus on your earthly journey as best you can every day; and when you can't, try to follow Him and affirm in your spirit that you can do all things through Christ who strengthens you (Philippians 4:13). Convince yourself like St. Paul [our great Christian saint and martyr], that by forgetting what is behind you [your past], and straining towards what is ahead, you must press on towards the goal to win the prize for which God has called you heavenward in Christ Jesus. "Living for Christ Jesus makes life worth living," said September 9th, 1999 issue of "Our Daily Bread." Just let God's Holy Word full your mind, rule your heart, and guide your tongue, and you will always be tremendously blessed—as you worship, praise, and give Him thanks, and all the honor and glory.

Consequently, I ask you to let these memorable verses of "Our Daily Bread" September 1999 issue, haunt your mind:

(a) "You can be confident about tomorrow [or the future] if you walk with God today" (Sept. 2nd, 1999).

(b) "For time and eternity, Jesus is all we need" (Sept. 11th, 1999).

(c) "Life's challenges are designed not to break us, but to bend us towards God" (Sept. 13th, 1999).

(d) "A changed life is the result of a changed heart" (Sept. 17th, 1999).

(e) "Why we are here is important; where we are going is most important" (Sept. 18th, 1999).

(f) "In every desert of trial [and temptation], God has an oasis of comfort" (Sep. 25th, 1999).

(g) "Christ is the bridge over the chasm of sin" (Sept. 26th, 1999).

(h) And, "It's not too late to make a fresh start with God" (Sept. 27th, 1999).

"Blessed be God forever!"

8

GOD'S ETERNAL HEAVENLY REWARDS AND GLORY, FOR THE OBEDIENCE OF THE REDEEMED AND THE RIGHTEOUS

In Romans 8:25, in the NIV Bible, St. Paul says, "If we hope for what we do not yet have, [our heavenly reward of eternal life and glory], we wait for it patiently." (With faith, hope, and the joy of the Lord, which is our strength).

Now, how do St. Paul and other born-again believers like me know and feel so very sure about that? It's only because of God's awesome and powerful spirit within us, and the Holy Spirit's presence also within us. How else can we get to know that? Holy Scripture says that God's ways are not like men's ways, and are past finding out. Therefore, God's spirit and the power of the Holy Spirit in man is so very awesome, that it searches and reveals all thing—even the deep and hidden secrets of God, says 1 Corinthians 2:10.

Just as the natural man understands the things and thoughts of natural man by the spirit of man within him, likewise, only God's spirit and the Holy Spirit can understand the things of God (1 Corinthians 2:11-13).

So when we receive the spiritual gifts of God's redeeming love and mercy, through His sanctifying grace and justification, with the power of Christ Jesus and the Holy Spirit after our conversion, we become spiritual vessels that God can use for his honor and glory. And then, God speaks to us and uses us powerfully for His kingdom ministry, because we are no longer children of darkness, or Satan's pawns. We become God's spokesmen and spokeswomen, and mediums or channels of His secret spiritual truths, His revelations, and His mighty works (or miracles). Therefore, St. Paul says to those who possess God's secret spiritual wisdom, and miraculous works and revelations, (or hidden truths), in 1 Corinthians 2:7-9—which does not refer to this present age, but to the future glorification of the redeemed and righteous in heaven: " [I] speak of God's secret wisdom that has been hidden and that God destined for our glory before time began. None of the rulers of this age understood it, [the crucifixion of Our Lord and Savior Jesus Christ], for if they had, they would not have crucified the Lord of glory"—so that we would not be destined to receive the reward of eternal life and glorification in heaven, after Adam and Eve sinned in the Garden of Eden.

Therefore, St. Paul affirmed and concluded about our heavenly rewards and glorification, in 1 Corinthians 2:9: "No eye has seen, no ear has heard, no mind has conceived, what God has prepared for those who love him." And, even though this is not explaining it too much, Holy Scripture also says in Psalm 16:11, that we will experience the "fullness of joy and pleasures forevermore." This means that there will be a great joyous celebration (or rejoicing) in heaven among the angels, and the saints (known as the redeemed and the righteous), more than when a repentant sinner on earth has been saved. So our joy will be full, complete, and eternal, and not like the temporary happiness induced by the influence of illicit drugs, alcohol abuse, illicit or corrupt sex, gambling, witchcraft, etc., etc.

The Holy Bible says that on Judgment Day, the redeemed and the righteous, dead and alive, will not experience the great end-of-time tribulations and torments that the unrighteous and Satan and his disciples will go through. And the redeemed and righteous dead in Christ will rise first; and those who are still alive will be caught up to meet Jesus Christ in the clouds with great glory, praise, honor, and power—"The Great Rapture." They shall see their "Great Redeemer and Lord" face-to-face, and they will experience no more crying, sickness, and no more pain. All earthly sicknesses and other Satanic afflictions of depression, worry, lack, fear, anxiety, guilt, condemnation, despair, blame and shame, persecutions, trials, temptation, and accusations of God's people by Satan, will be no more; and God will wipe away all the tears from their eyes. They will bask in the victory, brightness, and glory of Christ Jesus, "The Lamb who was slain" and is now "The great Conquering Lion of Judah."

9

CONCLUSION

The awesome powers of the redeemed and the righteous human souls on fire for God are so very incredible most times, that only when or by summoning our indwelling faith in God and invoking the wisdom and power of the Holy Spirit and Christ Jesus, we can remove the dark cloud of doubt and unbelief in our intellect, to clearly see, understand, accept, and appreciate, God's power at work, in and through the redeemed and the righteous—presupposing of course that we first accept these two basic biblical truth-principles below:

(a) "With God all things are possible" (Matthew 19:26, NIV); and,

(b) "Everything is possible for him who believes" (Mark 9:3, NIV).

So that God's awesome manner of providing "abundant-life" for all born-again believers, through their faith in Jesus Christ, and their power to control some supernatural phenomena just like Jesus, will not seem so very "far-fetched."*

Most times, the unbeliever can't, will not, or refuses to understand and/or accept, the powerful godly gifts vested in the redeemed and the righteous, because he, (the unbeliever), views, judges, and understands them as ordinary, plain, and simple persons—and not as persons with God's anointing. Therefore, most unbelievers or unrighteous persons believe that every miracle the redeemed or righteous perform, and their good fortune or blessings, are as the result of chance, luck, fate, magic, or the use of occult activity. Even more strange and incredible to the unbeliever today, is the account of the prophet Elisha's dead or lifeless body performing miracles, as stated in 2 Kings 13:20-21, in the Holy Bible. Such an incredible power!

God's redeemed and righteous human souls on fire for Him are not ordinary people. They are an anointed people who are Holy Spirit-filled, faith-filled, and commissioned with the power of and by Jesus Christ himself (Matthew 28:18-20; Mark 16:15-18). And they communicate with God continually—day and night—as Psalm 1:1-2 implies. They are spiritual power-houses. So 1 Peter 2:9, in the NIV Bible, says about them:

> "But you are a chosen [or special] people, a royal priesthood, a holy nation, a people belonging to God, that you may declare the praises of him who called you out of darkness into his wonderful light. Once you were not a people [no one important], but now you are the people of God [a special people]. Once you had not received mercy, but now you have received mercy [or redemption]."

And 2 Timothy 1:7, in the NIV Bible, also says about them, "God did not give us [the redeemed and righteous] a spirit of timidity [or fear], but a spirit of power, [including boldness and courage], of love, ['agape love'], and self-discipline [or self-control, or a sound mind]."

"For the weapons of our warfare are not carnal, but mighty through God to the pulling down of strongholds [especially Satan's]; casting down imaginations, and every high thing that exalteth itself against the knowledge of God, and bringing into captivity every thought to the obedience of Christ" (2 Corinthians 10:4-5, NIV).

Therefore, Isaiah 54:17, in the NIV Bible, says to them, "No weapon forged against you will prevail, and you will refute every tongue that accuses you. This is the heritage of the servants of the Lord, and this is their vindication [or protection] from me, declares the Lord."

These above facts really summarize the incredibly awesome inherited powers and privileges of the redeemed and righteous human souls on fire for God, for performing their kingdom ministry on earth, as God's Church militants.

To all "God's Church militants"* on earth for Christ Jesus I say, (using St. Paul's words), "May the God of hope fill you with all joy and peace as you trust in him, so that you may overflow with hope by the power of the Holy Spirit"--the hope of and for eternal life rewards in the hereafter--(Romans 15:13, NIV).

And, "Let the people [the redeemed and righteous of the Lord] praise thee, O God; let all the people praise thee. O let the nations be glad and sing for joy...." (Psalm 67:3-4, NKJV), "For the joy of the Lord is our strength" (Nehemiah 8:10, NKJV), "....You [we] shall go out [into ministry] with joy, and be led forth in peace; the mountains and hills will burst into song before you [us], and all the trees of the field will clap their hands," says Isaiah 55:12, NIV.

"So let's just praise, give thanks, and bless the Holy Trinity!"

In closing, I hope that every new believer in Christ Jesus who have read this handbook will be so filled with God's Holy Spirit, that he or she will want to share with others and say like Jeremiah and I: "His word is in my heart like a fire, a fire shut up in my bones. I am weary of holding it in; indeed, I cannot" (Jeremiah 20:9, NIV).

"May God be blessed and praised!"

GLOSSARY AND PHRASE LIST

A

A BACKSLIDER: A born-again believer in Christ Jesus, who has forsaken the way of righteousness by returning into the world, to practice sin.

A BACK-UP PLAN: A rescue plan for if the first or original plan did not or does not work out.

A CHILD OF GOD: A born-again baptized believer in Christ Jesus, who lives righteously.

A CHRIST-REDEEMED SOUL: One who has been saved or set free from the power of sin by Christ Jesus.

A CLEAN SLATE: It means that there is no more evidence for condemnation: freedom from all blame or accusations.

A CONDEMNED SINNER: A sinner who has not been justified by God.

A CONVICTED SINNER: A sinner who was hell-bound because he practiced sin, but was suddenly accused and arrested by the power of the Holy Spirit's conviction.

A GENERATIONAL CURSE: An evil trait or curse which a person inherits from his/her ancestors.

A NEW CREATION: A spiritually, intellectually, and physically transformed person.

A NORM: An accepted form of social or cultural behavior.

A PARABLE: A story told by Jesus in the Holy Bible, to illustrate and teach good morals.

APOSTLES: The specially chosen, trained and anointed disciples of Jesus, for God's earthly Kingdom ministry.

ASIA MINOR: The cities of biblical times in south west Asia, around the Mediterranean Sea, where St. Paul and other New Testament time Christians did ministry for Christ Jesus.

B

BACKSLIDERS: Check the definition of a backslider in "section A."

BLOOD-WASHED: Saved and sanctified (or cleansed) from sin, by the power of the precious shed blood of Jesus on Calvary's wooden cross.

BORN-AGAIN: Like a seed that has been sowed in the ground, then dies and sprouts to "new life," every new Christian is supposed to die to self, selfishness, and sin, (the old self), and then be regenerated (or have new life through the power of Christ Jesus).

BOUNCE-BACK: To recover from a problematic situation, and return to one's normal or former functioning self.

C

CALLED: To hear the voice of God beckoning to you by name.

CHOSEN: To be specially singled out or selected by God.

CHRISTIANS:	Born-again believers who are Christ-like— which means, they have the disposition of Christ Jesus.
CHRIST-LIKE:	Exhibiting the character (or mind, heart, and spirit) of Christ Jesus.
CONVERSION:	The whole process of turning away completely from sin through repentance, after Holy Spirit conviction and God's justification, to embrace righteousness through Christ Jesus.
CRUSADES:	Open-air evangelical camp-meetings.

D

DEMONS:	They are Satan's rebellious cohorts or fallen angels from heaven, who support and do all his evil biddings.
DEMON-POSSESSED:	People whose mind and actions are controlled by Satan.
DIVINE INTERVENTION:	Situations where God takes over and exercises His control or divine will.
DIVINE ORDER:	All situations where there is God's influence of peace, harmony, divine justice, unity, stability, love, and right outcome (or righteousness).
DRUG BARONS:	Persons who traffic (or sell and process) illegal drugs as a career, and live affluently on or off its returns.

E

ETERNAL LIFE:	A life without end.
EXHORTATIONS:	Encouragements.

F

FAR-FETCHED:

Seemingly unbelievable, or unreal.

FASTING:

To abstain from food or some regular bad habit, and engaging in fervent prayer, to achieve particular positive spiritual benefits.

FOOLS FOR CHRIST:

Those people who are (most times), very ignorant and innocent about many worldly matters, but are very wise and inquisitive about most good spiritual matters.

FRUIT OF THE SPIRIT:

Check Galatians 5:22-23, in the Holy Bible.

G

GENERATIONAL CURSE:

The revolving curse of God for sin, which all humanity inherited from Adam and Eve (our first parents). It can only be cancelled or broken by our faith in Jesus Christ who saves, and in His shed precious blood on Calvary's cross, which has the power to cleanse us from all unrighteousness.

GOD'S ANOINTING:

God's special favor and consecration with holy oil, for those whom He has specially called, chosen, blessed, and sent out into the world to do kingdom ministry.

GOD'S CHOICE:

God's special selection, followed by recognition and favor.

GOD'S CHURCH:

All of God's specially chosen and anointed people, who rally together, work together, and stay together in one accord, to have and express fellowship with one another for God's kingdom ministry on earth.

GOD'S CHURCH MILITANTS:

God's anointed church people on earth, who wage warfare against Satan and his disciples, for God's kingdom, "in the name of Jesus."

GOD'S FAVOR: God's unmerited blessings of his grace and mercy to and for us, through Christ Jesus.

GOD'S HOLY WORD: Holy Scripture.

GOD'S JUSTIFICATION: Our exoneration for or from sin, through God's grace and mercy.

GOD'S SHAKINA GLORY: God's manifestation of His inexpli cable awesomeness, power, and majesty.

GOD'S SPECIAL ANOINTING: God's special consecration with holy oil, along with His favor and power, for per forming His kingdom ministry.

HE (God) IS SOVREIGN: He is Lord, ruler, and master of our lives.

HIGH PRIEST: The Priest who occupies the highest office in the Jewish temple, and would enter the most holy place on the day of atonement— once a year—to offer sacrifices for the sins of his people, and then himself.

HE IS LORD: A specially venerated and honored person: a distinguished person.

HIS LOVING-KINDNESS: Check Psalm 103:1-18, to know all about God's loving-kindness.

HIS RESSURECTION EXPERIENCE: Jesus died, was buried, and de scended to hell to witness to all the imprisoned spirits of the dead who died before he came, and resurrected. He took the keys of hell from Satan, and arose triumphantly after three days in the tomb. Death, sickness, lack, evil, and Satan, could not hold him down as a prisoner in the grave; for He arose triumphantly on Easter morning with a healthy, glorified, and im mortal body—meaning that He conquered Satan, and the power of death, sin, sickness, and hell, which man feared. Therefore, by His stripes—the cruel tortures, pain, punish ment, bloodshed, and suffering which He endured for our sake, to free us from Adam and Eve's generational curse—we are healed, cleansed, and delivered. By His death and resurrection experience we have complete victory and power over Satan. Satan is now a defeated foe who can't harm the redeemed and righteous anymore—un less God allows him to do so, as in Job's case, in the book of Job. The redeemed and the righteous human souls on fire for God are therefore powerful Church militants, be cause of Jesus Christ's resurrection-experi ence for us.

HUMBLE REPENTANCE: Feeling truly sorry for and acknowledging one's sin or sins, and making a sincere effort to forsake it and begin a newly sanctified life.

IMMORTAL: Meaning that you or it can never die.

J

JESUS CHRIST'S CHURCH MILITANTS: The born-again redeemed and righteous human souls on fire for God, who fight for the cause of righteousness, through the power of Christ Jesus and the Holy Spirit.

JESUS CHRIST'S GREAT COMMISSION: cf. Matthew 28:18-20, and Mark 16:15-18.

JESUS CHRIST'S SAFETY-FENCE: Check page 20, Chapter 1, section 2c.

JUDGMENT DAY: The end of time (or last day of humanity), when Jesus Christ will return in glory with His angels, to judge all creation, both living and dead.

JUSTIFICATION: God's exoneration of a sinner.

JUSTIFIED:	Freed from all blame, shame, and punish ment.

K

KINGDOM MINISTRY:	God's assigned task or tasks of love and service for a called, chosen, and anointed born-again believer, which has spiritual sig nificance and motives, and qualifies him or her as a kingdom worker.

L

LORD OF THEIR LIVES:	Master and ruler of their lives.

M

MAN'S NATURE:	Man's inherent human tendencies or inclinations.
MEDITATION:	The art and act of elevating one's mind, heart, spirit and soul, by listening to God with faith, through reading and/or ponder ing on a spiritual issue, magazine, or Holy Scripture, in silence and in solitude.
MERCY:	The art and act of forgiveness.
MESSED-UP:	In a helpless and hopeless situation.
MONEY LAUNDERING:	The act of spending money to promote cor ruption (illicit sex, illegal drugs, alcohol abuse, etc.).
MORALS:	Whatever pertains to right and wrong

N

NEW LIFE:	A rebirth, or spiritual regeneration.

O

OMNIPOTENT:	All powerful.

OMNISCIENT:	All knowing.
OUR ADAMIC NATURE:	Humanity's old sinful or criminal nature in herited from Adam and Eve.
OUR LORD AND Our PERSONAL SAVIOR:	king, ruler, protector, provider, teacher, counsellor, problem solver, and Only Way for Salvation.

P

PARABLES:	Stories with a hidden meaning, told by Jesus in the Holy Bible, to illustrate a moral teaching.
PASS-THE-BUCK:	Passing your problems on to someone else to solve for you.
PENTECOST:	A Jewish festival kept on the fiftieth day after the second day of the Passover: the feast of Whit Sunday.
PERSONAL SAVIOR:	See the information under "O" about "Our Lord and Personal Savior."
PRAYER:	The art and act of talking to God with reverence, in silence or aloud, whilst lifting up your heart, mind, soul and spirit to Him, "in spirit and in truth."
PUBLIC SPECTACLES:	Worldly exhibition of self or talents.

R

REBELLION:	An illegal physical protest or uprising, such as Satan did in heaven.
REDEEMED:	set free by a price paid.
REDEMPTION:	The act of buying back, through making amends for the sinful soul—a ransom for deliverance.

REPENTANCE:

Showing perfect contrition (or sincere sorrow) for sin, by humbly confessing it to God, and then forsaking it completely.

RESURRECTED:

Risen from death to life.

RIGHTEOUSNESS:

Living a life of faith in and obedience to God, through the power of Christ Jesus and the Holy Spirit.

S

SAINTS:

Redeemed sinners who live a life of right eousness.

SALVATION:

The process of being saved (or delivered from sin), through the conviction of the Holy Spirit, and trusting and believing in and on the power of the shed blood of our Lord Jesus Christ on Calvary's cross, to cleanse us of all unrighteousness..

SANCTIFICATION:

The cleansing process from sin, by the power of the shed blood of Jesus for us on Calvary's cross, and subsequent continual life-time conviction by the Word of God, and the power of the Holy Spirit.

SANCTIFIED:

Cleansed from all unrighteousness.

SATAN'S PAY-ROLL:

Satan's illegal rewards and benefits for all those who partake in any special unrighteousness.

SAVED:

Redeemed by Jesus' shed blood on Calvary's cross.

SAVIOR:

One who sets another person free by paying a special price (or ransom).

SCENARIO:

A life situation in which persons are actors as in a dramatic play.

SIN:

Willful disobedience or rebellion against

	God's laws.
SOVEREIGN:	Supreme in power, like a king.
STRONGHOLDS:	The areas of human refuge where sin reigns, and Satan is in control.
SWEPT UNDER THE CARPET:	Like an issue dismissed and not recalled, or not mentioned again, as though not important.

T

TESTIMONIES:	Statements made to establish or prove a point, or some fact or facts.
THE APOSTOLIC CHURCH:	God's Church, founded on the faith and tra dition of the apostles, in Christ Jesus.
THE BRETHREN:	All baptized born-again believers in Christ Jesus.
THE BLESSED TRINITY:	The triune or three persons, who constitute or make up the God-head: the Father (God), the Son (Jesus Christ), and the Holy Spirit.
THE CHRIST-REDEEMED SINNER:	A sinner saved by the grace and mercy of God, and the power of Christ Jesus.
THE CHURCH'S MILITANTS:	The redeemed and righteous body of be lievers on earth, who live for Jesus Christ by witnessing, teaching, and proclaiming the "Good News" of His Gospel message of sal vation and eternal life; and that salvation can be found in no other name under heaven but Jesus Christ alone.
THE GENTILES:	The non-Jewish or pagan people (or na tions), who were not considered initially as part of God's salvation plan, before Jesus Christ came on earth to die for all sinful humanity.
THE GODLY JUSTIFIED:	Those persons exonerated from their sin or

	sins by Almighty God.
THE GOOD NEWS:	Jesus Christ's gospel message of salvation.
THE HOLY OF HOLIES:	That part of the Jewish temple (or Syna gogue), which was visited only once a year, by the Jewish high priest, to intercede with God for His chosen people (Israel) of biblical times.
THE MOSAIC LAW:	The laws which God gave to Moses on Mount Sinai, to govern His biblically chosen people: the Ten Commandments.
THE NEW DISPENSATION:	God's law of grace and mercy, operating through faith in Christ Jesus.
THE OLD DISPENSATION:	The Mosaic Law.
THE ONLY WAY, TRUTH AND LIFE:	That is who Jesus is.
THE PLOW:	A piece of farm equipment for cutting fur rows in the soil: a symbol of God's tool for performing service or work in His vineyard (the world).
THE REDEEMED:	One who has been "set free from sin" and "washed (or cleansed) by the Blood of Jesus."
THE SINNERS PRAYER:	It is the acknowledgement and confession of one's sin to God with one's mouth, with humble and contrite belief in Jesus Christ in one's heart and mind, and trusting and ac cepting Him as one's Lord and Personal Savior.
THE SYNOPTIC GOSPELS:	The gospels of the four evangelists (Matthew, Mark, Luke, and John).
THE TRUTH:	Reality.
THE UNREDEEMED:	Those who are lost in trespasses: because they have not believed in, acknowledged,

accepted, and confessed, Jesus Christ as
their Lord and Personal Savior.

TO ATONE: To make amends.

TONGUES: A special Holy Spirit induced language called
                         "Glossolalia," which only God and certain
                         specially gifted Holy Spirit-filled Christians
                         can understand and interpret.

TO SHINE: To live righteously, or be a true example of
                         holy living.

TRANSGRESSIONS: The breaking of God's law.

TRUTH ISSUE: A reality situation or issue.

W

WORKERS OF INIQUITY: People who practice wickedness on earth.

Y

YOKE: A burden, sin, or affliction.

YOUR CROSS: A problem or yoke.

BIBLIOGRAPHY

A Gardener's Little Devotional Book: Worthy Inspired Publishing Group. Copyright. USA. 2014.

Authorized King James Version (1978): *The Holy Bible*: Printed by World Bible Publishers in the USA.

Barclay, W. 1977: *Ethics in a Permissive Society*. Made and printed in Great Britain in Font Paperbacks.

Barker, K., Burdick, D., Steck, J., Wessel, W., Youngblood, R., (Editors): *The NIV Study Bible*. USA. 1995.

Bosworth, E. F. *Christ The Healer*: Whitaker House Publishers. Copyright. PA, USA. 2000.

Brogle G. De. *Revelation and Reason*: Burns & Oats, London, England. 1965.

Daily Devotions: A collection of inspirational thoughts and images. Copyright. Was first published by Paragon in the UK in 2011.

Daily Word: November 24th issue, 1986. USA.

Fitzmyer, J. A., Murphy, R. E., (Editors): *The Jerome Biblical Commentary.* London, England. 1969.

Good News Bible: American Bible Society. Copyright. USA: 1966, 1971, 1976; 1979.

Our Daily Bread: November 24th issue, 1986. USA.

Our Daily Bread: July—August issue, 1988. USA.

Our Daily Bread: January 16th issue, 1989. USA.

Our Daily Bread: September—October issue, 1999. USA

Sydnor, William: *More Than Words:* Harper And Row Publishers. Copyright. USA. 1990.

AFTERWORD

When I had almost finished this spiritual hand-book, Satan attacked me with stress, doubt, fear, and sciatica pains, to steal my health and joy in the Lord. So I quickly gave myself to fervent prayer, meditation and fasting.

At one point in time I could not bear the sciatic pain anymore, so I went down on my knees and humbly cried out aloud to God, "My God, my God, why have you forsaken me!" And, as I did that, I remembered a verse in the "Ancient and Modern" Anglican Church hymnal—written by William Cowper—which says, "Satan trembles when he sees the weakest saint upon his knees." So again and again, I cried out aloud to God on my knees: "My God, my God, why have you forsaken me!"

Suddenly, the Holy Spirit made me recall these verses of Holy Scripture:

> (a) "Do not be afraid—I will save you. I have called you by name—you are mine. When you pass through deep waters I will be with you; your troubles will not overwhelm you. When you pass through fire, you will not be burned; the hard trials that come will not hurt you. For I am the Lord your God: the holy God of Israel who saves you" (Isaiah 43:1-3, GNB).

(b) "No weapon forged against you will prevail, and you will refute every tongue that accuses you. This is the heritage of the servants of the Lord, and this is their vindication from me," declares the Lord. (Isaiah 54:17, NIV)

(c) "For God hath not given us the spirit of fear; but of power, and of love, and of a sound mind" (2 Timothy 1:7, NIV).

(d) "Listen! [said Jesus], I have given you authority, so that you can walk on snakes and scorpions and overcome all the power of the Enemy [Satan], and nothing will hurt you" (Luke 10:19, GNB).

(e) "Do not grieve, for the joy of the Lord is your strength" (Nehemiah 8:10, NIV).

(f) "Not by [human] might nor by [human] power, but by my spirit, [supernatural power], says the Lord Almighty" (Zechariah 4:6, NIV).

(g) "God is at work in you, both to will and to work, for his good pleasure" (Philippians 2:13, NIV).

(h) Therefore St. Paul says, in Romans 8:37, NIV, "In all things, we are more than conquerors."

(i) And in Romans 8:28, NIV, he said, "And we know that in all things God works for the good of those who love him, who have been called according to his purpose."

Finally, after praying, fasting, and meditating on the above scriptures, my Pastor came and prayed with me and anointed me with olive oil; and my health was restored immediately (James 5:13-15). That is why the Letter of James, chapter 5, verse 16, says: "The fervent prayer of the righteous has a powerful effect." Supporting this axiom, Jesus said, in Matthew 18:19-20, GNB, "And I tell you more: whenever two of you on earth agree about anything you pray for, it will be done for you by my Father in heaven. For where two or three come together in my name, I am there with them."

So, whenever Satan presents you with a negative thought or difficult situation that you can't handle, "pray and rebuke him in the name of Jesus;" and cast your burden on Him (Jesus). Then place your problem or burden at the foot of Calvary's cross as "something for Jesus to do" (SFJTD). Jesus will solve it for you, and the Holy Spirit will help you to recall the right and positive scriptures to mind, that will comfort and strengthen you. Then, Satan will flee from you and you will have peace.

Deuteronomy 8:3 says, (NIV),"Man does not live on bread alone, but on every word that comes from the mouth of God." That is how God, Jesus, and the Holy Spirit, nurtured me back to joy, peace, good health, boldness, grace, and wisdom. Therefore,

I am very thankful to the Blessed Trinity for restoration. May the Holy Trinity be praised, blessed, thanked, worshiped, and indefinitely glorified, for their loving-kindness to me. Satan's works were subdued and nullified, by the power of two united, redeemed and righteous human souls on fire for God.

"Let us praise and bless the Holy Trinity at all times!"

ABOUT THE AUTHOR

Culbert D. Blenman was born in Vieux-fort, St. Lucia, in the Caribbean, (W.I).

He did his spiritual studies at the Roman Catholic Theological Seminary of St. John Vianney, and the University of the West-Indies St. Augustin campus in Trinidad, simultaneously.

Subsequently, he became a high school teacher/missionary and Sports Director overseas, before returning home in 1973.

Once at home, (St. Lucia), he transitioned to the Anglican (or Episcopal) Church in 1981, where he had a conversion and healing experience, after having a personal encounter with Jesus Christ and the Holy Spirit. So he became a born-again believer in Christ Jesus then.

Four years later, he was ordained a licensed Lay Reader and Minister, to serve all three Anglican Churches in the south of the island of St. Lucia, W.I.

After serving there for 23 years, he finally realized that God was calling him to complete his conversion experience, by having proper water baptism just like Christ Jesus did. After all, Jesus Christ should always be a believer's role model.

With the Holy Spirit's counsel and guidance during fervent prayer, meditation, and fasting, he resolved his water-baptism issue by having it done, at "Born Again Revival Tabernacle Church." God is truly awesome and works in mysterious ways: Even though His will for an unbeliever is past finding out, it is not always so for most born-again believers in Christ Jesus. For the Holy Spirit (our helper) always counsels, consoles, teaches, guides, directs, and leads believers along the right path. And, as the Holy Spirit and God guides and directs a believer continually, he or she is better able to makes wise choices and decisions, that will enhance his or her life, and God's Kingdom ministry.

Culbert D. Blenman is now a retiree who presently does ministry for Christ Jesus, by engaging in "world-wide outreach evangelism," through his inspirational writing—because he is very mindful and aware that Jesus Christ has specially commissioned all His apostles, disciples, and every other born-again believer, to go out into the whole world and preach "The Good News" of His gospel message of love, salvation, and eternal life, to all nations (Mark 16:15).

"Let us exalt and bless His holy Name!"

www.ingramcontent.com/pod-product-compliance
Lightning Source LLC
Chambersburg PA
CBHW020856090426
42736CB00008B/394